Praise for *Spc*

"This compelling, highly original novel from an internationally renowned sociologist and author brings us to a meeting of people with radically different perspectives and life experiences who are asked to collaboratively answer a question. We eavesdrop on their lively discussions, explore the beauty of Iceland with them, cheer as we see them help each other conquer personal fears, and rejoice as they bond into a caring community. People with very different ideas can learn to learn and care for each other. Kindness matters. We need each other's ways of knowing. *Spark* is perfect for any group—class, family, community—where differences need to be respected and commonalities affirmed. If I ran the world, I would make this book required reading."
—Laurel Richardson,
Distinguished Professor Emeritus of Sociology,
The Ohio State University

"Leavy's work has profoundly affected the graduate students in my program. *Spark* will surely have a deep impact. I can think of no better way to launch discussions about epistemology, ontology, and the research process more broadly, and to expose students to fiction as a social research practice. I was captivated throughout as I, too, pursued an answer to 'the question.' *Spark* is brimming with insightful reflections, not only about research, but also about life. I plan to use it in all of my research courses as a required text."
—Ricardo D. Rosa, School of Education,
University of Massachusetts Dartmouth

"Award-winning author Patricia Leavy has done it again—written an arts-based research novel that I couldn't put down! Amid breathtaking Icelandic landscapes, the characters and the challenge they are grappling with come to life. This book should be used in sociology, psychology, communication, and other classrooms, touching on themes including methodology, small groups, diversity, and leadership. Students will love Leavy's creativity, skill in character development, and ability to take them where they may not have previously journeyed, both geographically and interpersonally.

Thought-provoking, intriguing, and clever, *Spark* left me wanting to live in the world that Leavy has created—a world of beauty and possibility."

—Robin Patric Clair, Department of Communication, Purdue University

"This intriguing novel illuminates the blinding force of presumptions—about one's own capacities, about other people, and, not least, about the 'requirements' of legitimate intellectual inquiry. Perhaps more fundamentally, it is about the possibility of transcending oneself, seeing people for who they truly are, and thinking beyond disciplinary silos. By freeing the creative imagination from its too-tight borders with the help—and even love—of others, this novel suggests, we can fashion new worlds of meaning and value."

—Mark Freeman, Distinguished Professor of Ethics and Society, College of the Holy Cross

"I have often utilized Leavy's books in my graduate social work courses. The characters in her novels expand the thought processes of new social workers on topics related to race, sexuality, and privilege. *Spark* has surpassed expectations. One of the strengths of this novel is how it promotes conversations about intersectionality as it relates to privilege. I am eager to share this remarkable work with my students."

—Renita M. Davis, Interim Chair, Troy University School of Social Work

"Delightful and thought provoking, *Spark* is a compelling read, whether in or out of the classroom. The novel follows the meeting of a very diverse group of people, with very different opinions and ideas of the world. It's through these characters and ideas that Leavy encourages the reader to leave all biases at the door."

—Taylor D., undergraduate, Raritan Valley Community College

"Leavy brings all of her creativity, craft, and insight to a novel that not only is an enjoyable read but also truly sparks layers of meaningful conversations. A diverse cast of characters is brought together to dive into answering one question. Through this process, readers are invited to explore the intellectual terrain of their own assumptions and biases. What is significant about *Spark* is how it so beautifully brings each character—and reader—to comprehend how we all arrive at answers that truly matter. Here is a novel that can accompany any class in research methods; it is exemplary of what it means to be multi- and transdisciplinary while celebrating each approach with deep respect. Be prepared to have your ideas spark and grow!"

—Celeste Snowber, Faculty of Education,
Simon Fraser University, British Columbia, Canada

"In this clever and captivating novel, Leavy shows us how a research project is collaboratively developed from the spark of an idea to research purpose to execution. This is more than a textbook—it is the story of how a group of artists and intellectuals with different skills become a cohesive research team. They must learn how to work with their differences and across research paradigms to see new ways of thinking and to trust in the research process. *Spark* represents the best of arts-based research from a master of fiction-as-research-method. I will be teaching this book in my undergraduate and graduate classes."

—Sandra L. Faulkner, Professor of Communication
and Director of Women's, Gender, and Sexuality Studies,
Bowling Green State University

"Leavy, one of the leading voices in arts-based research methods, has penned an engaging novel that illustrates for new scholars the different ways that diverse people come to understand the world— and understand it together. *Spark* does as its title suggests, kindling readers' openness to other people, other ideas, other ways of seeing and being. Modern societies need this skill set more than ever. Through archetypal characters you'll recognize—either in yourself or in people you have met and worked with—and a richly described setting at once alien and familiar, Leavy teaches key research processes that might be used to tackle even seemingly intractable problems. Students will find the novel to be a gentle, entertaining introduction to the research mindset, with vivid characters, dialogue, and scenes that can serve as springboards for deeper, more grounded discussions than those afforded by a traditional textbook. The suggestions for creative writing, classroom use, and research activities provide hours of follow-up opportunities to help turn the novel's spark into a burning excitement for cooperative research." —Marcus B. Weaver-Hightower, Professor of Educational Foundations and Research, University of North Dakota

"A thoroughly enjoyable and thoughtful read! Seven brilliant thinkers from diverse disciplines and countries have just five days to answer a deceptively simple question. This beautifully written novel, set in Iceland's magical landscape, draws readers into a puzzle the group must solve, while simultaneously exploring characters' personal struggles. The gradual peeling back of layers, intriguing premise, realistic dialogue, and abundant food for thought make *Spark* not only a page turner, but also an intellectual treasure that will stick with me." —Christine Sleeter, Professor Emerita, College of Professional Studies, California State University, Monterey Bay

"*Spark* shows how we can think differently yet connect through understanding. Reading about a group of people with diverse backgrounds and viewpoints who come together as the story unfolds is captivating in such a polarizing time. Leavy's characters and their journey show that sometimes the question is more important than the answer. This novel truly has something for everyone." —Corey P., undergraduate, Fairfield University

"I just finished reading this breathtaking book in one sitting, pausing only for a much-resented phone call interruption. This is the perfect book for first-year students for so many reasons. It's a story about arriving at a place that you think is awesome but possibly too big for you, judging everyone's outsides against your insides, and finding the power of community, context, and perspective. It's about becoming more aware of how you typically understand (or misunderstand) others—and learning to listen, to tolerate uncertainty, and to try new things (some of which won't work). This is a sensational book that should be everyone's freshman read." —Eve Spangler, Department of Sociology, Boston College

SPARK

Also from Patricia Leavy

Contemporary Feminist Research
from Theory to Practice
Patricia Leavy and Anne Harris

Handbook of Arts-Based Research
Edited by Patricia Leavy

Research Design:
Quantitative, Qualitative, Mixed Methods,
Arts-Based, and Community-Based Participatory
Research Approaches
Patricia Leavy

Method Meets Art, Second Edition:
Arts-Based Research Practice
Patricia Leavy

Handbook of Emergent Methods
*Edited by Sharlene Nagy Hesse-Biber
and Patricia Leavy*

SPARK

PATRICIA LEAVY

THE GUILFORD PRESS
New York   London

Copyright © 2019 The Guilford Press
A Division of Guilford Publications, Inc.
370 Seventh Avenue, Suite 1200, New York, NY 10001
www.guilford.com

Printed in the United States of America

This book is printed on acid-free paper.

Last digit is print number: 9   8   7   6   5   4   3   2   1

Library of Congress Cataloging-in-Publication Data

Names: Leavy, Patricia, 1975– author.
Title: Spark / Patricia Leavy.
Description: New York : The Guilford Press, 2019.
Identifiers: LCCN 2018025304| ISBN 9781462538157 (pbk.) | ISBN 9781462538164
    (hardcover)
Subjects: | GSAFD: Suspense fiction.
Classification: LCC PS3612.E2198 S66 2019 | DDC 813/.6—dc23
LC record available at https://lccn.loc.gov/2018025304

*To my friends from
the Salzburg Global Seminar Session 547,
real-life superheroes*

Contents

a spark exists
within, between, among
and within that spark,
entire worlds of possibility

Chapter 1

* * *

Balancing her suitcase on the escalator, Peyton scanned the row of drivers as she descended into the arrivals gate. *Oh thank God, there's a driver holding a sign with my name on it.*

"Welcome, Professor Wilde."

"Oh, thank you. Please, call me Peyton. I'm so relieved to see you."

"Why is that?" he asked.

Suddenly realizing she couldn't possibly tell him she feared this trip was a horrible mistake or some sort of scam, she fumbled over her words. "Oh, uh, just a long trip."

"My name is Aldar. Please follow me to the van."

"Aren't we meeting the others?"

"No. Most arrived in the middle of the night. You're my only early morning pick-up. More arrive in a couple hours."

"I see."

As they approached the van Peyton slipped a crumpled piece of paper with her travel agent's emergency contact information into her pocket. Her palms were sweaty from clenching the paper, and she casually wiped them on her coat.

"Please, relax and enjoy the ride to Crystal Manor. Shall I put some music on?"

"Okay."

He turned the radio dial on and flipped to a contemporary station. "Ah, this is perfect to acquaint you with our part of the world."

As Björk started swirling in Peyton's head, she leaned back, trying to ground herself. In the days before the trip, her concealable, low-grade anxiety had risen and started bubbling out. *I'm not good with new people. How did I get myself into this?* She had contemplated canceling. *A family emergency? Illness?* Her excuses all seemed lame. *How could I live with letting this chance go? How could I look in the mirror?* In the end, the prospect of a free trip to Iceland, surrounded by "some of the greatest thinkers of our time" was too intriguing.

But it was more than that. As a girl, Peyton lived in a state of hopeful anticipation. Great things were just around the corner. Magic fell like the snowflakes she attempted to catch on the tip of her tongue. At the age of seven her mother took her to a concert to see their favorite singer. There was a moment she would never forget, a moment that she clung to. Just as the lights went out, everyone sprung up from their seats and cheered. A surge of excitement coursed through her body. Her heart raced. She threw her arms up and cheered too. As the audience stood screaming, they were all connected. She was a part of something exquisite in that moment— the moment between the lights going off and the music beginning. A lump formed in her throat and tears of joy flooded her eyes, and the show had not yet begun. From that moment forward, Peyton lived with a lump in her throat, excited for what was coming and how she might be a part of it. Life was big, filled with the kind of possibility that has you leaping toward each day. There were math classes, chores, household arguments, visits to the dentist, bullies on the playground, bad moods, and other dimensions of life, but they didn't diminish her hope. Curious whether other people felt the same tug at their hearts, she became fascinated with audiences. At movies or the occasional play or dance performance, she was always reprimanded by her father. "You're looking the wrong way. Face forward," he said, poking her arm. She never understood why he couldn't see it wasn't the dancers on stage, but the faces of those watching that were most extraordinary. Over time she trained herself to "face forward." Perhaps that was her mistake. She studied sociology in college and pursued a career as a professor, hoping to instill sparks of inspiration in others, but by her thirties her belief in the bigness of life had faded. The pit in her stomach had passed. Aliveness was elusive. Her belief in "what if?" had packed a bag, seeking greener pastures.

By all accounts her life was enviable. She was a professor at a liberal arts college and a published author. She lived in a safe, gorgeous community in Vermont. Recognizing her many privileges, and not wanting to appear ungrateful, she never said a word to anyone about her loss of hope. Loneliness set in. Her anxiety grew. She became uncomfortable around others. The smallness, the tediousness of life that she once rejected, had come to seem inevitable. At work, the reverberation of a simmering anxiety never abated.

The day the invitation arrived was impossibly ordinary. She was delivering a lecture to her theory class that she had given two dozen times before. Most of her students hadn't done the assigned reading. As had become the norm, she continued on with her lecture, observing that Anna was online shopping, Celia was updating her social media, and Tom was asleep in the corner. She said nothing. Later, during a dreaded department meeting, her colleagues bickered about core requirements and teaching loads. Peyton stared out the window wishing to go unnoticed, much like her students whose complacency no longer troubled her. She stopped at the grocery store on the way home to pick up a prepared meal. At the register, the cashier, Harold, talked her up as always.

"What'd you get tonight?"

"Chicken."

"Watching a movie?"

She shrugged, unsure if he made awkward conversation with everyone or if this was an attempt at flirting. It didn't matter.

When she arrived at her apartment building, Mrs. Goldsmith was struggling to manage her cane while retrieving a package in the vestibule.

"Here, let me," Peyton said, picking up the package.

"Oh, thank you. Always such a nice girl," Mrs. Goldsmith said.

Peyton carried the parcel into Mrs. Goldsmith's first-floor apartment.

"Would you be a dear and help me open it?" she asked.

Peyton nodded and opened the package. Mrs. Goldsmith looked pleased with the contents, a pink dress and cardigan set she had purchased from home shopping.

Peyton let herself out and returned to the vestibule to collect her own mail. She entered her apartment, changed into sweats, and poured a glass of Beaujolais. She was about to take her meal into the living room to Netflix something when she decided to sort the mail. In the middle of a pile of bills and brochures, there it was: the invitation.

Dear Professor Wilde,

Congratulations! You are among forty-nine gifted individuals worldwide that have been selected to participate in a five-day seminar in Iceland, in a seaside town outside of Reykjavik. This event has been underwritten by the Goodright Foundation. We will pay for all of your travel expenses and provide complimentary food and lodging at the spectacular Crystal Manor, a luxurious private estate and hotel. You will spend your time here engaged in structured discussions with your colleagues, some of the greatest thinkers of our time. You will also have opportunities to explore our unique landscape, referred to by many as the land of "fire and ice." We have planned special excursions designed to inspire and create lasting memories. Participants will be divided into groups and given one question to answer during the duration of their visit, the results of which will be distributed among numerous think tanks aimed at global education, cultural enrichment, scientific research, peacekeeping, and social betterment. We can't overstate the importance of the results to emerge from this process. Your participation is vital to the success of the program. We do so hope you will accept our invitation.

Sincerely,
Gwendolyn Goodright, Director

She was lost in thought, remembering how thrilling it was receiving the invitation, when Aldar surprised her saying, "We are arriving. Those are the gates."

She sat straight up and looked out the window. *I can't believe my eyes. It's extraordinary.* As they slowly wound down the drive the pristine manor revealed more of herself rising from the trees, behind her, water clear as glass, with mountains in the distance so defined they appeared as a cardboard Hollywood set.

"Welcome to Crystal Manor, Professor."

＊   ＊   ＊

"The main estate is on the left. That's where the dining hall, meeting rooms, and library are located. On the right we have a newer, more modest building, which is the hotel, where the guest rooms are located. Please, this way," Aldar said.

This is incredible, Peyton thought as she followed him into a side door marked "Check-In," which brought them to an unassuming reception desk.

"And this is where I leave you for now," he said, placing her suitcase on the floor.

She looked around but there wasn't a soul in sight.

"Don't worry, Fana will be here momentarily to check you in."

"Who?" she asked, but he was already gone. Looking at the door, wondering how Aldar disappeared so quickly she didn't notice when a beautiful, dark-skinned woman appeared behind the counter.

"Welcome, Professor Wilde."

"Oh, gee. You startled me. I'm sorry."

"My name is Fana," she said, smiling brightly. "I am Ms. Goodright's assistant. On behalf of the Goodright Foundation it's my great pleasure to welcome you to Crystal Manor. How was your journey?"

"Oh, fine, thank you."

"Very good. Here's your welcome packet. I'll escort you to your room so you can get settled and familiarize yourself with the information in your packet. Lunch will be served in the grand hall at one o'clock. That will be your first opportunity to get to know the other participants. Our intern, Diego, will provide a tour of the property after lunch and then will lead everyone to the main conference hall. Ms. Goodright gives her opening address at four o'clock. It is there you will be given instructions for the week."

Peyton nodded.

"Right this way," she continued. "You're on the second floor."

As they walked up the stone staircase, Peyton marveled at each detail: cherubs carved into the banister and lettering she couldn't decipher.

"Your room is right down here."

"Uh huh," she muttered, enthralled by a statue of what looked like a mystical creature.

"Here we are, room 2-7," she said, unlocking the door. "Please, after you."

The room was charming. A bed dressed in cloud-like bedding, a long chest of drawers, and a small writing desk, which sat before the windows. Fana opened the white drapes revealing a view of green and blue as far as the eye could see.

"Your bathroom has been prepared with amenities but please don't hesitate if there is anything you need. Dial the number one on your telephone for the front desk," she said, handing Peyton the old-fashioned skeleton key. "There is a map of the property in your welcome packet. Lunch and all of the scheduled events are in the main estate. We look forward to seeing you at one o'clock in the grand hall. Of course you are welcome to explore the grounds and main estate as you wish."

"Okay. Thank you, Fana."

Fana smiled before quietly letting herself out.

This is so strange. How did I wind up here? Don't do that, Peyton. Don't question it to death. Just be grateful and enjoy it.

Her thoughts were interrupted by a knock on the door.

"Yes? Did you forget something?" she asked as she opened the door. A young man with a mop of dark brown hair was before her, holding a tray with silver vessels and a vase of purple flowers dotted in white.

"Greetings, Professor Wilde," he said in a thick accent. "I'm Diego."

"Oh yes, sorry. I thought it was Fana. She mentioned you."

"I'll be giving everyone a tour after lunch. I've brought you a snack in the meantime. May I?" he asked, tilting his head.

"Goodness, yes, please come in."

"I'll set this over here on the desk."

"Thank you."

"I'll see you after lunch, Professor."

"Please, call me Peyton."

He smiled. "Chau."

"Are you Italian?" she asked.

"Chilean."

"Chau."

＊　　＊　　＊

Hungry after traveling, she inspected the tray—a beautiful fruit platter, cheese, a slice of ginger loaf, water, tea, and coffee. *They think of everything.* She poured a cup of coffee and nibbled on some fruit and the moist cake before remembering she was supposed to study her welcome packet. She picked it up, noticing a label on the top corner with her name and the number 2547-7. *Hmm.* She opened the folder to find a typed letter atop a large packet.

Dear Professor Wilde,

It is our great pleasure to welcome you to Crystal Manor. You are one of forty-nine participants carefully curated for this event. We ask you to take this responsibility seriously. Your participation is vital to the success of our foundation's mission. We hope you will see that we have spared no expense to provide participants with everything needed— nourishment, comfort, inspiration—to stimulate productive reflection.

In the enclosed packet you will learn about each of the forty-nine participants. Photographs are included. While you will have time to get to know all of the participants during meals and other informal time, structured meetings and excursions will occur in groups of seven. Information about the members of your group can be found on the second to last page. Your group's itinerary is on the last page.

Professor Wilde, you have been assigned a special role. One member from each group is designated the scribe. At the end of the seminar, the scribe alone is responsible for providing a written response to the question you are charged with answering (which will be revealed at the opening address). Observe carefully, listen to your colleagues, trust your intuition, and don't be afraid to change your mind. You needn't consult the group at the end of the five days. The final report is solely in your hands.

Wishing you a productive stay,
Gwendolyn Goodright

A special role . . . the scribe alone is responsible . . . the final report is solely in my hands. Why me? As she started learning about the other participants, flipping from page to page, reading each biography, one more distinguished than the next, her worry grew. A world-renowned chemist from India who had received his country's highest honor in science; an award-winning classical composer from Austria who was one of Deutsche Grammophon's top-selling artists; the most successful political cartoonist in the United States with over forty awards and two hundred magazine covers to his credit; and on and on. *How did I get selected for this? I'm just a normal professor with a book that sold merely a few hundred copies. I don't fit in here. What were they thinking? Maybe it was a mistake. What will the others think of me?* Panic set in. She began to feel hot. A sharp pain coursed through her stomach. "Oh my God, I'm gonna be sick," she said aloud before scurrying into the bathroom. Eventually, with a settled stomach, she returned to the bedroom, grabbed the packet, and slid into bed. Propped against two pillows, she turned to the second-to-last page to learn who was in her group.

Liev: a renowned Russian neuroscientist whose theory of how brains process new information made him the most cited contemporary scientist in his field. His work has been translated into more than thirty languages.

God, he looks like Professor X from the X-Men. It's intimidating. Who's next?

Ariana: a well-regarded emerging Peruvian neuroscientist with more than twenty publications and grants in excess of a million dollars.

She's young to be so accomplished. Pretty too. I wonder if it's hard being a young female in her field.

Dietrich: a German philosopher whose analysis of Nietzsche changed the thinking and teaching across the field, garnering him a host of international awards.

He looks so serious, like he never smiles. Maybe it's just his glasses. I shouldn't prejudge.

Ronnie: an American visual artist who pioneered a new style of 3D collage that led to solo exhibitions at the MoMA, Tate Modern, and Musée National d'Art Moderne.

Funny, I always think of artists being eccentric but she's innocuous looking and kinda nerdy.

Harper: an Australian children's dance teacher. She runs a small studio in Melbourne.

Hmm, that's kind of a regular job, but she is in the arts, which is cool. She's really stunning. I'd kill for flowing blonde hair like that. I bet she lives on a beach. She has that look.

Milton: an American farmer who won Blue Ribbons at fairs and farmer's markets across New England for his organic produce including his unique hybrid radishes.

Hmm, a farmer. That's different. That's a regular job too. He looks sweet. Kind of old to come here alone. Must be at least seventy. Wonder what a farmer could possibly add to a group of scholars and artists. But even he's won awards. Why am I here? I'm just a sociology professor at a school no one's heard of. My students didn't even read my book. I wonder if it's because of that New York Times op-ed. That was just dumb luck. Stop obsessing, Peyton. You were invited just like everyone else.

She flipped to the last page to see a detailed itinerary. Breakfast was from eight to nine o'clock each morning. They had personal time each day from six to seven, followed by dinner. It was suggested everyone attend "nighttime opportunities for socializing" after dinner. The days were entirely structured with "brainstorming sessions" in designated locations, excursions (one day to the Golden Circle and another to the Blue Lagoon), a buffet lunch, and afternoon tea.

Tired from the travel and with her head spinning with information, she decided to take a short nap before lunch. Paranoid about oversleeping, she set both the alarm on her phone and the one in her room for noon. Nestled under the comforter, she closed her eyes. Before drifting to sleep Peyton had one clear thought: *What am I doing here?*

Chapter 2

*   *   *

*I*t's not a dream; it's real, ran through Peyton's head as she reached to turn off the alarms. After freshening up, she stared at her reflection in the mirror. *I'm in a mansion in Iceland. It's a once in a lifetime experience. There's nothing to be nervous about. I hope I don't get lost though. I have no sense of direction.* Suddenly worried the grand hall could be difficult to find, she glanced at the map and headed out.

Once at the main estate, she knew she was going the right way when she saw familiar faces from her welcome packet wandering down the same hallway. Uncomfortable meeting new people, she started to feel a little anxious, when a spirited voice said, "You're Peyton, right?"

She turned to see a petite woman with short dark hair and a big smile. "Yes. And you're Ronnie, right?"

"I sure am," she said as she outstretched her hand. "Glad to meet you. When I saw your profile I was excited to have you in my group."

Peyton assumed she was being polite and smiled awkwardly.

"Looks like the grand hall is right up there," she said. "Can't wait to see it. This place is really something, isn't it?"

Peyton nodded.

"Have you seen the library yet?" she asked.

"No, I went right to my room when I arrived."

"If you're a book person, it's a dream. I know they're giving us a tour later, but I couldn't help but poke around. My ancestors must have been explorers, who knows, I love seeing new places."

"That's probably why your art is so innovative."

Ronnie smiled.

"From what I read about your collage work you see things in new ways. It takes a curious mind to do that. An explorer of sorts."

"See, I told you I had a feeling about you. I knew we'd get on famously!"

Peyton smiled. Her heartbeat slowed and her anxiety passed.

When they arrived at the grand hall, Diego greeted them. "Nice to see you, Ronnie and Peyton. Please, go in and help yourself to lunch and meet the other participants. And if there's anything I can do to make your stay more comfortable and to facilitate your important work, please let me know."

"Thank you. We sure will," Ronnie said before turning to Peyton, "Let's sit together."

"Sure," Peyton replied, offering Diego a smile and head tilt as they passed by.

"Holy cow!" Ronnie exclaimed upon entering the aptly named grand hall. They stood for a moment looking up at the hand-painted ceilings, at least thirty feet above. There were rows of large round tables, intricately carved from dark glossy wood, satin-lined chairs, and crystal chandeliers dripping like frozen rain. Mammoth windows lined the far side of the room, revealing the water. It was breathtaking.

People milled about, helping themselves to a sprawling buffet.

"Should we grab some chow?" Ronnie asked.

Peyton nodded.

As they inspected the impressive array of offerings, each with a card indicating allergens—smoked fish, shrimp, turkey, a carved roast, locally foraged mushrooms, salads, cheeses, whole fruits, and pastries—Peyton said, "I shouldn't have eaten that ginger loaf. It was delicious but I'm not very hungry. Did you eat that?"

"I have celiac disease. Can't eat gluten. Diego brought gluten-free cake to my room, but I passed."

"It must be hard having a food allergy," Peyton said, placing a slice of smoked salmon on her plate.

"It's only tough when I travel. Buffets are tricky. Cross-contamination is a killer."

"Oh, I wonder if they could bring you something from the kitchen."

Just then a member of the wait staff came over. "Ms. Richmond, my name is Juliette and I am head of the dining staff. As you can see we have placed allergen information on the buffet. Today everything is gluten-free except for the roast and of course the pastries. If you have any concerns or special requests from the kitchen please let me know. We have rice crackers and gluten-free bread in the kitchen that we can bring you at any time."

"Thank you." Then turning to Peyton, Ronnie said, "Told you this place was something."

Peyton smiled.

After they finished making their selections, they scanned the room. Clusters of people were seated at each table, some whom Peyton recognized from her welcome packet. Ronnie walked toward a half-filled table, and Peyton followed.

"Hi, there. I'm Ronnie and this is Peyton," she said as she took a seat. They met a physicist from India—warm and friendly, Peyton liked her immediately; two South American literature professors engaged in their own conversation; and Milton, the New England farmer in their group. Peyton sat between Ronnie and Milton.

Carafes of Icelandic water and fresh juices, as well as pots of coffee and tea, were set at the center of the table. Ronnie, quite short, had to stand and lean in to reach the water, which she then passed to Peyton.

"So, what's your story?" Ronnie asked the physicist after taking a forkful of tuna salad. From there the conversation took off. Peyton tried to engage Milton, but he responded with one-word answers. She couldn't tell if he was shy or out of his element. She sat admiring Ronnie's ability to make conversation with strangers, taking in the details of the room, and above all watching the participants. She looked at who people sat with, talked to, and their expressions as they perused the buffet. Some were impressed while others acted as if this was commonplace. Mostly she watched each person's demeanor. Liev, the neuroscientist, came in with Ariana in tow. He walked fast with his shoulders high, unimpressed by this place. *Is he confident or arrogant?* Peyton wondered.

People were finishing their coffees and helping themselves to more pastries when Diego asked for everyone's attention. "I hope you enjoyed lunch. I'd like to formally introduce you to the staff who are here to assist should you have any special dietary needs."

He introduced the staff, each person in full uniform. Peyton was amazed by how every detail was attended to and no expense spared. *And even Diego said our work here is important. I wonder what they'll have us do,* she mused.

"Please feel free to bring your snacks and follow me."

As they huddled closer together, following Diego, Peyton and Ronnie met more participants. Ronnie introduced herself to anyone nearby and introduced Peyton by extension. First they were taken to a multi-faith prayer room. It was a humble room with stone walls. "Please feel free to visit this space anytime you wish. As noted in the contract you signed when you agreed to participate in this seminar, we ask only that you are respectful of one another. We value cultural, religious, and spiritual differences among our guests," Diego said.

They continued on and saw several magnificent sitting rooms, each with its own theme and color scheme, and a table surrounded with chairs or in some cases loveseats. They were set up for conversations, missing only the participants. Notebooks and pens were laid out on each table. Diego informed them these were the meeting rooms. Peyton's favorite was the Japanese garden room, which had parquet floors, white wallpaper with pink and green flowers, and stunning antique furniture, including two ornate wooden sofas covered in light green silk facing each other, matching chairs at either end, an oval table with inlaid wood in three shades, and gold lamps with paper-thin silk lampshades. People asked questions about the furnishings and the history of the estate. Diego was a wealth of information and promised they would learn more from Ms. Goodright. Peyton was fascinated by the paintings lining the hallways, landscapes unlike any she had seen before. There were bodies and faces in the clouds, rolling hills, mountains, and lava rocks. She thought she was imagining it until Ronnie whispered, "Look how the snow mimics a human form on those mountains. Do you see that?" She then raised her voice and said, "Hey, Diego, what can you tell us about these paintings?"

"They're a private collection, made by Icelandic artists, owned by the foundation. This is their permanent home. When the foundation was established here they wanted to support the local art community. The three on that side are by Kjarval, a famous twentieth-century painter. Nature is a prominent theme in Icelandic art, and he traveled around the country. He had the idea to present Icelanders with work that might help them see surprises in their own environment. After your excursions to the local sites I'm sure you'll begin to understand why nature inspires creativity."

Diego continued the tour. "You've obviously seen a lot of art, have you seen paintings like this before?" Peyton asked Ronnie.

"Variations. Different cultures have their own versions, but I haven't seen any quite like these. See, in that one, the mountains are bodies, but it's completely integrated. I mean, they're also straight up mountains."

Peyton considered her words as they strolled into the next room, which Diego called "the music hall." It was a medium-sized room with wood beams running along the white ceiling. A Bosendorfer piano sat in the corner, and an upscale version of dark wooden picnic tables with benches lined one side of the room.

"Sometimes we host performances and lectures here. We move the tables and put rows of folding chairs and a podium. We have a few planned for you. You may also use this space during the eve-nings as a place to relax and enjoy one another. You can bring drinks from the pub," Diego said.

"The pub?" someone asked.

"Yes, please follow me down the back stairs."

Ronnie smiled at Peyton as the group made their way down the narrow, winding staircase. The pub had a dungeon quality that charmed everyone. With low ceilings, the oval-shaped room with gray stone walls and tile floors felt intimate and less grandiose than the rest of the manor. The right-hand wall was lined with high-top tables and stools. On the left there was a fully stocked bar, includ-ing a small closet with potato chips and other snacks, a sizable rack of red wines, and coolers filled with beer, white wine, prosecco, and assorted nonalcoholic beverages.

"Is there a bartender?" Liev asked.

"No. Everything is self-serve. Staff members stock the pub dur-ing the day. In the evenings it is reserved for uninterrupted guest use," Diego replied. "Now please, come see the game room, through that archway. We have a pool table, table tennis, and a few video games."

Ronnie leaned close to Peyton and whispered, "Seems like they want us to make the most of our downtime."

"Uh huh," she replied. *Great, more pressure. I'm horrible at min-gling. I wonder if it would matter if I just went to my room each night after dinner.*

"There is one final room to show you. It is my personal favorite so I always save it for last. Let's return upstairs," Diego said.

Minutes later they entered the library. It was beyond a fairytale: glossy wood floors, antique furniture, and walls lined high with books as far as the eye could see. Old-fashioned wooden ladders hung on the racks, allowing one to climb all the way to the hand-painted ceiling to retrieve a special tome. Everyone was in awe, even Liev, who plopped down on an ornate loveseat covered in blue vel-vet. He smiled, surveying the room.

People kept looking upward while, from the center of the room, Diego began speaking. "We consider the library the jewel of Crystal Manor. I'm sure you can see why. Our collection includes books from every discipline across subject matter. The art and world history collections are particularly robust. We're most proud of our extensive offering of translations, allowing the words of thinkers from across the globe to live within these walls. First editions can be found in the glass cases. Please, take some time to browse. You may borrow anything you like. Naturally we use an honor system, no formal checkout. Our library is open twenty-four hours a day for your pleasure."

"I'm heading to the art stacks," Ronnie said. "Want to come?"

"I think I'm just going to meander," Peyton replied.

Ronnie headed off with focus while Peyton slowly walked along the book-lined walls, skimming titles and brushing her hands along old leather book spines. Suddenly there appeared to be a hidden door built within the shelves. Diego came up beside her, smiling like a schoolboy.

"Is this a secret door, like in the movies?" she asked half-jokingly.

He laughed. "Come, I'll show you."

He removed a key from his pocket and opened the magical little door. They entered the small, dark space to find a spiral staircase. He pulled a string, dimly illuminating the space and causing her heart to flicker. "It goes to the roof. We keep it locked for safety, wouldn't want anyone stumbling around up there after a night in the pub," he said.

"Ah, no, you wouldn't want that."

"No one goes up there, not even the staff. Shame, really, the view is spectacular."

"I bet."

"We should return. I need to get everyone to the main conference hall for the opening talk. Please take a moment to go to the far side of the library, to look out the windows. You'll see it's quite special."

He tugged the string, darkening the room, and they emerged from the hideaway. Peyton headed to the windows.

He's right, she thought. Stretching before her, blue Icelandic water pure as new love, leading to a horizon of mountains that looked like chocolate cupcakes swirled with mint icing. She turned back to the enchanted library, and then back again to the water. *Nirvana, this place is truly nirvana.*

*   *   *

The conference hall was distinct from the rest of the estate: it was all business. Rows of rectangular tables, recessed lighting, and a podium all revealed the room's purpose. Pocket notebooks and pens were laid out for each participant. Peyton and Ronnie sat with a few people they hadn't met yet, including Harper. Tall with sun-kissed skin and shaggy blonde hair, her Bohemian sensibility was even evident in the casual way she draped her body in her chair. Ronnie immediately began chatting her up.

"I was excited to see there's another artist in our group," she said, "How long have you been running your dance studio?"

"A few years. I toured Australia with a small modern dance company for a bit before that. Got injured, and well, you know. Found a new path. I do love working with the children though. It's quite rewarding. Tell me more about your collage work. And Peyton, I don't mean to sound naïve, but what exactly does a sociologist do?"

Good question, she thought. Before either could respond their attention turned to the podium, where Fana stood tall and graceful. "Honored guests, once again, welcome to Crystal Manor. I do hope you are all settling in well. Now our work begins. I met Ms. Goodright several years ago, in my homeland, Ethiopia. At the time I was working as project coordinator at a human rights organization. The Goodright Foundation provided us funding for a special program near to my heart. Ms. Goodright came ostensibly to oversee the implementation of the program. I quickly learned she was simply there to offer a helping hand. We became friends and colleagues. A year later I was humbled to accept a new position working directly for the foundation, confident together we could do the most good for the most people. It is my great pleasure to introduce you all to a woman I respect deeply, our director, Ms. Gwendolyn Goodright."

Everyone clapped as Fana adjusted the microphone several inches lower. A petite woman with red ringlets framing her face popped up from the front of the room. Dressed in a black and white wrap dress, with rouge-stained lips, she possessed a timeless quality. She and Fana brushed hands as they traded places. New energy swept through the austere room. Peyton felt a joyful kind of anticipation. *There's a palpable lightness in the room,* she thought. *There is lightness in me.*

"Hello, and welcome," she said warmly. My name is Gwendolyn Goodright and on behalf of the Goodright Foundation I sincerely thank you for being here. As my name suggests, the foundation was started by my grandfather and his colleagues, in 1947. Seeking support from businesses, organizations, and heads of state across the globe, they started the foundation in response to the atrocities of World War II. Shocked by what they witnessed they asked, how does neighbor turn on neighbor, and what might be done to prevent such tragedy? How might we work together across differences to elevate humanity, to define ourselves? How might we move forward? And on the deepest of levels, what is humanity? What promise lives at our core? The foundation's way of being in the world has changed and evolved over time, but our commitment to the ideas of our founders has not wavered. I have proudly served as director for the past fifteen years."

The way in which she spoke exuded a warmth and earnestness that instilled a sense of purpose deeply into Peyton's spirit. She felt at once needed and grateful. A sense of possibility started to stir. For the first time in years she turned to see the audience, casually glancing around the room, examining everyone's expressions. *Do they feel it too?* she wondered. *They feel it too, at least some do,* she thought before returning her attention forward.

"People are often curious about how we came to make our home in Iceland. Our founders were Austrian, American, and Japanese by birth. They serendipitously met at a seminar in Berlin, became colleagues and comrades. Each was differently swept up in the aftermath of the war. My grandfather hailed from a wealthy family and procured the initial funding, but the vision was all of theirs. So when they sought a center of operations they first turned to their own backyards. They strongly considered Schloss Maximilianskron in Austria for its historic significance, an old mill in the United States, and several other locations. But when Mr. Yamamoto, an avid outdoorsman, visited Iceland, he told his colleagues he had found the future of the foundation. While our work could be carried out anywhere, he believed the purity of the water would inspire purity of thought, and the tumultuous landscape, the kind of gentle ruthlessness that gives rise to possibility. After a long process, they discovered Crystal Manor. Over the years we have expanded the property but never lost sight of the primacy of nature that drew us here all those years ago. We do hope you will take advantage of the grounds during your stay."

Several people asked questions about the estate, and then the moment was upon them. Ms. Goodright said, "As you know, we have divided you into seven groups of seven. You will work in your groups to answer one question."

Notebooks opened as everyone prepared themselves.

"Your question is as follows: 'What is the answer?'" Ms. Goodright stepped slightly back from the microphone, indicating she was done. She smiled as looks of confusion, and in some cases amusement, swept over the room.

Liev called out, "What is the question?"

"'What is the answer?'" she replied.

"Is this a joke?" he asked.

"The question is: 'What is the answer?'" she assuredly repeated.

"It's clearly philosophical," Dietrich shouted in Liev's direction.

"It's absurd," Liev responded. "I am a scientist. I assumed I was invited for my expertise."

"You were," Ms. Goodright responded.

Ronnie raised her hand. "Um, I see this is perhaps intended to be abstract, but are there more specific follow-up questions to guide us?"

Ms. Goodright shook her head, her perfect curls bobbing from side to side. "You have all you need. And I know you will be successful. We are counting on it. For now we have assigned each group a room in which to meet. Please consult your packet or the chart by the doors. You have an hour before your daily personal time and dinner. Introduce yourselves to each other. Tomorrow the real work begins. And to the scribes, do take careful notes. I'll see you again over the course of your stay."

With that, Fana escorted her out of the room as everyone sat there, dumbfounded.

*   *   *

"Well, what do you make of this?" Ronnie asked as they walked to meet their group in their assigned space, the library.

Peyton shook her head.

Harper chimed in, "I think this is going to be fun. It's wonderfully free-spirited to ask something so, so, uh . . ."

"Vague?" Ronnie asked.

Harper nodded.

"But they want a concrete answer. We need to figure out what they mean," Peyton said.

"Don't worry. I'm sure the others will have ideas. It's only day one," Ronnie assured her.

They caught up with Milton who had been slowly walking in front of them. "Milton, what do you make of the question?" Ronnie asked.

"Don't know," he said.

Soon they arrived at the library to find a small table in the center of the room, surrounded by a loveseat and five chairs. Dietrich was sitting in one of the chairs. Harper plopped down on the loveseat, removed her shoes, and crossed her legs. "Hi there, I'm Harper," she said, smiling at Dietrich.

"Pleased to meet you," he replied in monotone, his cheeks reddening ever so slightly.

Peyton sat next to Harper and gestured hello. Ronnie walked over, shaking Dietrich's hand before taking the seat closest to Peyton. Milton wandered around the room while the rest sat in silence. Nearly fifteen minutes passed before Liev and Ariana entered the room, engrossed in conversation. "Sorry, I had to make a phone call," Liev said.

Ronnie pursed her lips as Liev, Ariana, and Milton filled the empty chairs.

"So, what did we miss?" Liev asked.

"Nothing. We waited for you," Ronnie said.

"Ah, let's get started," he replied. "It's no secret I find this perhaps a bit ludicrous, but we are obligated."

Ariana visibly held back laughter demonstrating her agreement.

He's really a piece of work. He's dooming us before we begin, Peyton thought. *If the two of them are a tag team we already have a block of negativity. I wish Ronnie and I were in another group.*

"It's a real honor to be here," Ronnie chimed in. "The results of what we do here could have far-reaching impact and they've gone to great trouble. I think we should give it a good go."

"Being open is everything. Let's embrace our imaginations and see where they take us," Harper added.

Liev crinkled his forehead, clearly annoyed.

"How should we start?" Ronnie asked. "Maybe we could go around the room and introduce ourselves."

"Didn't you read the welcome packet? There's a description of everyone in it," Dietrich said matter-of-factly, adjusting his glasses.

"Well that's hardly intimate," Ronnie replied. "We're going to be together all day every day this week. We should talk about ourselves in our own words. Maybe everyone could share something about their work and something more personal that's not in our bios."

"Something funny or embarrassing, or a hobby perhaps," Harper suggested.

"Fine. I will start," Liev said. "I'm a neuroscientist and it's too complex to explain my theory to you, but I research how the human brain processes new information. It was not as was thought for decades. Basically I challenged the common wisdom in my field. They tried to ignore me, silence me, bashed me even. But my theory was correct so eventually they had to take me seriously. I've won many awards for my work."

Holy shit. Who talks that way about themselves? Peyton thought.

"Tell them something personal about yourself," Ariana said softly.

"Ah, yes. I'm a wine enthusiast. I travel in Europe quite a bit giving lectures and I always enjoy the fine red wines. I abhor cheap wine."

"We have wonderful wines in Australia. You can actually get a beautiful white very inexpensively. Nothing like enjoying a bottle of crisp white wine with friends. On a hot day, you know?" Harper said.

Liev ignored her and turned to Ariana. "Your turn," he said. Before she could open her mouth he addressed the group, "This is my protégé, Ariana."

"Uh, yes. Hello everyone," Ariana said, visibly uncomfortable. "I am also a neuroscientist studying how the human brain processes new information. I'm from Peru and met Liev when I was in graduate school, after which I traveled to Moscow to work with him. Differing somewhat from his work, my research focuses specifically on how the human brain processes creative work, specifically literary work, such as literature or poetry. Next year I'll be working in the United States with some colleagues at the National Institutes of Health on a grant we received. We'll be doing many things, such as taking brain scans as people read fiction. As for something personal, when I was young I had aspirations to be a standup comic. I've participated in some amateur nights at bars. It's a de-stressor. I don't think anyone in my professional life knows that."

Hmm. Maybe she's not so bad, Peyton thought.

"So, who's next?" Ariana asked.

"I'll go," Harper said. "I'm a dancer, primarily modern dance. Although I trained in classical ballet too. From Sydney originally, but now I live in Melbourne. In my spare time I do yoga to stay centered and nurture the mind–body connection. I also have a vegetable garden. I'm quite proud of it. Milton, I'll have to get some tips from you," she said, smiling.

"Well, I guess that's my cue," Milton replied. "I'm a third-generation farmer living in Southern Maine with my wife, kids, and grandkids. I'm nearly retired though. Mostly my sons take care of things, but I still pitch in and do my watermelon radishes. Frankly I don't know what I'm doing here, but it was my first chance to travel out of the country. My wife said I was too old to say no, so here I am."

"Good for you seizing the opportunity, Milton," Ronnie said. "Tell me, has your family been on the same land for generations?"

He shook his head. "Upstate New York. I moved to Maine in my twenties."

Ronnie opened her mouth but before she said anything Milton smiled and turned to Dietrich, "You're up I think."

Dietrich adjusted his glasses and cleared his throat. "Uh, yes, fine. Hello, I am Dietrich and as you know I am a philosopher. I was very intrigued by the invitation to come here. Now that we have been given our mandate I see I will be of use. The question is purely philosophical. In terms . . ."

Liev interrupted. "You cannot say it is philosophical. I've given it some thought and it is a research question. Scientists are here for a reason."

Ariana nodded.

Dietrich shifted in his chair. "Surely you could understand the question . . ."

Ronnie interjected. "Hey folks, I think we're getting ahead of ourselves. We're supposed to start tackling the question tomorrow."

"Let's get to know each other," Harper added.

"If he says something like this you can't expect me to be silent," Liev said, gesturing toward Dietrich.

Dietrich shifted in his seat again. "Ronnie is correct; we should leave the question for tomorrow. I apologize," Dietrich said. "I only meant to introduce myself. Someone else should go now."

Harper smiled at him. "Tell us something personal about yourself."

Dietrich's nose twitched. "Uh, yes, okay. I love classical music. I guess that's something."

"Did you see there's a famous composer here? He is also a pianist from what I hear." Harper asked.

Dietrich nodded.

"Do you play an instrument?" she asked.

"No."

"I fiddle on the piano a bit," she replied.

After a moment of silence Ronnie said, "Well, I guess it's my turn. I'm Ronnie. I'm a visual artist. I dabbled for years in painting and sculpture until I discovered my passion for 3D collage. I love taking disparate elements and putting them together. My pieces are mostly large-scale installations based around various themes. For something personal, I'm a total foodie but I've got a food allergy so it's tricky. My wife is a great cook and has figured out how to make substitutes for all my favorites. Peyton, looks like you're the last one up."

"Hi everyone. I'm Peyton and I'm a sociology professor at a small liberal arts college. I mostly teach classes non-majors take to fulfill their social science requirements, like intro to sociology and social problems. As for something not in my bio, well, I'm scared of heights. I don't know why that came to mind. I guess that's it."

"You are the scribe for the group, correct?" Ariana asked.

Peyton nodded. "I don't know why they picked me. It's nerve-racking having the extra responsibility."

"It was probably random, who got assigned," Liev said.

"Yeah, probably," Peyton said. "I promise I'll take careful notes and represent the group thoughtfully."

"You'll be great!" Ronnie exclaimed.

Liev looked at his watch before announcing, "It's nearly our scheduled personal time. Should we call it a day? The serious work begins tomorrow."

Everyone agreed. As the group began to disperse Ronnie asked Peyton if she wanted to hang out in the library before dinner.

"I think I'm going to head to my room for a bit. I'll see you at dinner, okay?"

"Sure thing. I'm gonna browse the stacks to bring some books back with me in case jet lag keeps me up later."

Peyton smiled and headed out.

✳   ✳   ✳

Dietrich entered his room, closed the door, and leaned against the wall. He removed his glasses, put his hand over his eyes, and shook his head. He rubbed his eyes and put his glasses back on. He walked over to the radio and turned on a classical station. Truly honored by the invitation, he had been looking forward to this seminar, determined to be of value. After listening to Ms. Goodright, he was even more committed. He had witnessed the aftereffects of World War II, in both the shame and silence of his elders. The foundation's mission spoke to him and he wanted to be a part of it. Unfortunately, for all of his good intentions, Dietrich was socially awkward. He feared he had inadvertently gotten off on the wrong foot. Perhaps it was more. Liev pushed his buttons. Dietrich had had a twin brother, Helmut. Gifted in math and science, Helmut had dreamed of becoming a scientist, encouraged by his parents, who said he would be a famous scholar one day. Dietrich was bookish and shy. Helmut had been his only true friend. When the two were twelve years old, Helmut had been diagnosed with cancer. He had died before his thirteenth birthday. Heartbroken, Dietrich turned to religious texts seeking answers. In college he discovered philosophy. For him, it was a way to make sense of a world that otherwise felt random. He devoted all of his energy to his work. It was all he had and therefore, in his mind, it simply had to be of value. As he sat on his bed, Beethoven filling the air, he longed to begin the day again. He feared he antagonized Liev. Soon his thoughts turned to Harper, and how lovely he found her.

✳   ✳   ✳

With the responsibility of being the scribe weighing heavily on her, Peyton turned on her laptop to make some notes about her group. *Hmm, I didn't really learn much. Only the personal things they shared. And how difficult some of them are. The instructions said to "observe carefully" and "listen to your colleagues" so I'd better be safe and record everything just in case.* She opened up a new document and at the top she typed:

What is the answer?

Day One

Liev is a misogynist who likes expensive wine.

Staring at what she'd written, she thought, *Come on, Peyton, they're counting on you. Maybe I should try to separate what people said or did from my impressions.* She deleted the line about Liev and listed everyone's name. She made two columns: the first labeled "Observations" and the second "Impressions."

What is the answer?

Day One

	Observations	*Impressions*
Liev	likes fine red wine; late	arrogant and sexist
Ariana	amateur comic; late	not sure
Harper	does yoga; has vegetable garden	lovely and low key
Dietrich	likes classical music	too serious
Milton	never left the US before; retired	not sure
Ronnie	foodie but has food allergy	enthusiastic
Peyton	scared of heights	in over her head

As she sat looking at her notes, she wondered how this group of seven oddballs could possibly answer the question.

Chapter 3

"Over here," Ronnie hollered, waving at Peyton from a table in the center of the room. *It's even more beautiful at night,* she thought as she walked over, exchanging polite smiles with other participants along the way. Peyton joined Ronnie, Harper, Milton, and several participants from different groups.

"This is really something, isn't it?" Ronnie asked.

Peyton nodded.

Each table featured white lace tablecloths, votive candles, and several tea vases holding delicate white flowers surrounded by mossy greens. There were carafes of water, fresh juice, and wine at the center of each table. Milton reached for the water when Juliette scurried over with a pitcher in hand. "Please allow me. What's on the table is for your convenience throughout the meal."

Milton gestured awkwardly as she began filling crystal glasses.

"Ms. Richmond, please let me know if you'd care for any gluten-free bread or rice crackers with your meal."

Ronnie smiled. "I sure would love some crackers. Thank you."

Another staff member came over with bottles of wine, offering a choice of red or white. Ronnie and Milton declined. As Peyton took a sip of her Sancerre, Ronnie leaned over, "I'm not a big drinker. I'm always worried when I travel it'll mess with my sleep cycles."

29

"To be honest I usually don't drink in professional settings but I'm hoping it will calm my nerves."

"You jumpy about the work ahead?"

Peyton shrugged. "I tend to overthink things."

"Hey, don't worry. We're . . ."

"Sorry to interrupt, but the buffet is open. Shall we?" Harper asked.

As they stood in line looking at the opulent spread, Peyton was awed by the grandeur. There were pâtés, cheeses, salads, stew, beef tenderloin, herbed chicken, poached fish topped with caviar, vegetables, potatoes, and noodles on the main buffet, and an eye-catching display of breads and sweet confections on a smaller table.

"Everything looks delicious," Peyton said.

"Yeah, I'm pretty hungry. Haven't eaten much today," Ronnie said as she took a spoon of chopped liver pâté, a piece of chicken, and a scoop of vegetables.

Peyton reached for the tongs on the cheese platter when from out of nowhere Liev jumped in front of her. "I forgot the dressing when I was here before," he said as he grabbed a bottle labeled "vinaigrette."

Ronnie looked stunned that he had cut in front of Peyton without so much as an "excuse me."

"Are you ladies ready for tomorrow?" he asked as he slowly drizzled dressing on his salad.

"Uh huh," Peyton said. "It's an honor to be a part of this. I hope we're up to it."

Liev chuckled. "Yes, well carry on and enjoy your dinner."

"He's so rude," Ronnie muttered.

I wonder if he means to be, Peyton thought.

✳　　　✳　　　✳

Plates were being scraped clean when Diego reminded everyone, "You're free to socialize in the music hall and pub. Bring your desserts or snacks if you like."

People started meandering toward the pub, some taking left-over desserts from the buffet. Harper said, "Perhaps I'll get one of the fruit bowls to bring."

"Good idea," Peyton said. "Ronnie, are you going to the pub?"

"My stomach isn't feeling so hot. I'm going to stop in my room and I'll try to meet you there."

"Oh, I don't even know if I'm going. I . . ."

"Come on. Just for a bit," Harper said, now holding a large bowl of fruit.

Ronnie assured her. "It'll be fine. Go ahead. See you later."

Peyton acquiesced.

The women parted ways and soon Peyton and Harper bumped into Diego, walking toward them.

"Good, you're going to enjoy yourselves," he said.

"Won't you join us?" Harper asked.

He smiled, revealing dimples. "It's just for guests, but thank you."

"Ah, we won't tell. Come if you like," she responded.

He smiled again, bowing his head with appreciation. "I have to tidy up the stacks in the library and make sure the rooms are prepared for tomorrow. I hope you have great fun with your colleagues."

"Diego," Peyton said, "I wanted to ask you something."

"The bowl is a speck heavy. Meet me in the pub, Peyton," Harper said before walking away.

"Yes. How can I help you?" Diego asked.

"Have you worked here long?" she asked.

"For a year."

"And how did you wind up here, if you don't mind my asking?"

"After college I left Chile to go to Sweden for my master's degree in international relations. As a part of the program we must complete an internship, which can be done abroad. I learned about this institute and fell in love, so to speak," he said, blushing. "I was very fortunate to receive the position. There are many applicants. I'm extending my stay for a second year. I can't bear to leave."

He talks so sincerely as if this place is enchanted, like he's enraptured by it. It's lovely. Peyton smiled.

"Professor, ah excuse me, Peyton. May I ask you something?"

"Of course," she said.

"Do you not feel comfortable here?"

"Oh, uh, well," she stammered, embarrassed she was so transparent.

"Please, do not be offended. I ask because, well because . . ."

"Go on. Please, you can say whatever you're thinking."

"The look in your eyes is like . . ."

"Yes, like?" she prodded.

"Like you want to be here but you're not quite sure how to be here."

She looked down.

"I'm sorry, perhaps I didn't say that well."

"No, you said it perfectly. You're very perceptive, Diego. I'm a little anxious, I suppose. A great responsibility has been placed on us. Even more on me because I have to provide the final report. And, well . . ."

"You were chosen. In the time I have been here, I have not seen any mistakes. Trust that you are up to it. You all are."

She nodded ever so slightly, comforted by his faith.

They stood for a moment before Peyton said, "Well I should let you get to your work."

"And you should join the others in the pub."

❋   ❋   ❋

Peyton stood in the doorway, peering into the pub. She spotted Harper at a table against the wall, with a few others. Ronnie was nowhere in sight. Ariana came up from behind. "I stopped in my room for a minute. Are you heading in or out?"

"Oh, uh, I just got here too."

"Well let's go see if we can find a drink," Ariana suggested as she brushed past her.

Peyton followed. The room was chilly. People were behind the bar helping themselves to drinks, sitting at tables, and standing around. Some were quietly chatting. Peyton peeked into the connecting game room. Liev and another man were battling each other in Ping-Pong while a few others played pool.

"Peyton, grab a drink. Come sit. I saved a spot," Harper called.

Peyton walked behind the bar where she scoured the shelves and coolers before settling on a small bottle of sparkling water. "Ariana, you're welcome to join us."

"Thank you. I'm going to bring my wine into the other room. I like to watch the competition."

"Will you play the winner?"

"I'm very competitive. I'd like to challenge Liev to a game but I may wait for another night."

Peyton smiled and joined Harper's table. They were in the middle of a conversation about the institute. Everyone was impressed by the building, staff, and food. Over the next hour they talked a little about their jobs, prior travel, and how they looked forward to exploring Iceland. Harper leaned over to Peyton and said, "Hope Ronnie is feeling all right."

"Me too. I don't think she's coming, though, and I'm tired. I'm going to head out."

"Sleep well. See you tomorrow."

Peyton walked to her room replaying the day: the cold of the Icelandic air, the awe-inspiring sight of Crystal Manor, the dreamlike library, the fascinating characters milling about, and the succulent food that warmed her from within. *This is an extraordinary opportunity. I hope I can make the most of it.* Her thoughts drifted to Diego's words, *"You were chosen. I have not seen any mistakes."* She thought about his love for this magical place. He was bathed in its glow. She wondered if over time even a spark of that magic would live inside of her too.

Chapter 4

*　　*　　*

Peyton followed the sounds of clanking breakfast dishes. Exhausted after a restless night, desperate for coffee, she was nearly blinded by the morning sun flooding the dining hall. Juliette greeted her.

"Good morning. The espresso machine is over there, and there's regular coffee and black tea on each table."

"Thank you."

Peyton headed straight to the buffet. She helped herself to a bowl of steaming oatmeal, which she topped with fresh raspberries. She surveyed the room, spotting Ronnie, Harper, and Milton sitting together. Relieved, she made a beeline to them.

"Good morning everyone," she said. "Ronnie, are you okay? I wasn't sure if you were tired or didn't feel well."

"Sick as a dog. Sorry I didn't make it to the pub. I was in bad shape."

"Oh no, I'm so sorry," Peyton replied, reaching for the coffee-pot. "How do you feel now?"

"My stomach finally settled. I'm a little low energy after it all, but I'll perk up."

"Do you know what made you ill?"

"Could've been anything, but I'm guessing the crackers. Maybe they weren't gluten-free. I'm taking it real easy today. I just got a banana and hard-boiled egg from the buffet."

Peyton smiled, already pouring her second cup of coffee. Her smile broadened when she noticed Milton's plate piled high with cured meats, cheeses, dried fruits, bread, Danish, and a yogurt on the side.

He caught her eye. "I like a hearty breakfast. Most important meal of the day."

"Oh, yes. Uh, I was just thinking how delicious the pastry looks."

"My wife wouldn't be happy."

Harper chimed in, "But hey, what she doesn't know won't hurt her. Right, Milton?"

He smiled and sunk his teeth into the flaky dough.

"Peyton, you're a woman after my own heart," Harper said.

"Pardon?"

Harper gestured at her oatmeal. "Healthy is all."

"Did you stay much longer at the pub last night?" Peyton asked, taking a spoonful of her oatmeal.

"Nah. Not much longer after you left. You didn't miss anything."

Peyton glanced around the room. Fana and Ms. Goodright were by the door talking to Juliette. Fana was stunning in a charcoal gray pantsuit and crisp white shirt, accentuating her physique. Ms. Goodright wore a mid-length gray dress with a ruffled bottom that mirrored her curls. Peyton tried to be subtle and continue eating, but she couldn't take her eyes off of them, as they walked over to the table nearest them, and minutes later to the table next to hers.

Peyton realized her table was next. She casually sipped her coffee, while the others carried on with their conversations. Everyone hushed when the women approached.

"Good morning," Ms. Goodright said. "I hope you're all feeling rested and well fed."

Everyone nodded and muttered politely.

"We wanted to wish you good luck as you begin your journey together. The urgency of the work you are carrying out places a heavy burden on your shoulders, and we do greatly appreciate your effort. We do everything we can to support your comfort. The organizations we work with look forward to your report."

"We're sure excited to get started," Ronnie said.

"Wonderful. Please, enjoy your breakfast."

"According to the daily itinerary, we're supposed to meet the others in the Japanese garden room in fifteen minutes. We better chow down," Ronnie said.

Anxious and exhilarated about what lay ahead, Peyton took a bite of her oatmeal, hoping to soothe the lump in her throat.

✳   ✳   ✳

Harper flicked off her shoes and plopped down cross-legged on one of the sofas. Peyton and Ronnie sat next to her. Liev and Ariana sat on the sofa across from them, and Dietrich and Milton each sat in a chair. Peyton grabbed a small notepad and pen from the table. Everyone looked at each other. Ariana broke the silence. "So, how do you think we should begin? I see they've put a large pad on an easel for us. Perhaps we should start by writing the question."

"Good idea," Ronnie said. Others nodded.

Ariana stood up and in black marker wrote: "What is the answer?" at the top of the board. She returned to her seat.

Liev spoke immediately. "It is clear we all have ideas about this. We should go around the room and each state our positions. Get it all on the table. Maybe there are agreements in the room. If there are competing ideas, we can begin to debate."

Ronnie looked flabbergasted. "Maybe we should frame it as a discussion, not a debate. Pretty early in the game to make it contentious."

"I'm with Ronnie," Harper said. "Let's all talk openly."

Liev rolled his eyes. "We need to look for hard truths. Facts.

Scholarly achievement results from rigorous critique. That's how it is done. You can't be sensitive about it," he insisted.

"A little sensitivity goes a long way," Harper responded.

"And no one said the question or our approach has to be scholarly," Ronnie said, making air quotes when she said "scholarly."

"I agree," Peyton said.

Liev opened his mouth but Ariana jumped in. "We can agree that we should begin with the question, correct?"

Everyone nodded.

"Let's go around the room briefly as Liev suggested, sharing our initial thoughts. I will make notes on the pad. Then we can see what we have and determine how to proceed. All right?"

Everyone agreed.

"Who begins?" Liev asked.

"Dietrich had some strong feelings yesterday. Let's hear from him," Harper said.

Dietrich smiled so subtly it was almost imperceptible. "Ah, yes. Well, okay," he said, shifting in his seat. He proceeded to explain why he felt the question was philosophical and must be answered by philosophical theorizing. One by one each person followed, offering his or her thoughts about the question and how best to answer it, except for Milton, who abstained.

Gesturing to the easel beside her, Ariana said, "Let's see what we have here. Dietrich thinks the question is philosophical, Peyton thinks it is social, Ronnie and Harper think it is intentionally abstract and we must ponder why. And Liev and I think it's a research question and we must determine how to apply the scientific method."

"Yup, that sums it up," Ronnie said. She then paused, looking like she was in distress. She tried to continue. "So how should, how should, uh . . ."

"What's wrong, Ronnie?" Peyton asked. "You look pale."

Ronnie leapt up. "I'll be right back. Sorry," she said, scurrying to the door.

"Gee, hope she's not sick again," Harper said.

"How do we proceed?" Dietrich asked. "Defend our positions?"

"Well, that won't get us far," Harper responded.

Ariana returned to her seat next to Liev. "We all responded to the question based on our field of study," she said. "I think . . ."

Liev interrupted. "That's expected. It does not change the facts. This is why we should debate to find the correct point of view."

For the next hour and forty-five minutes they debated whether or not to debate. Their discussion was interrupted by a loud chime followed by an announcement over the intercom: "The first segment has ended. You have a fifteen-minute break. Please take a walk or help yourself to the refreshments set up in hallways and common spaces outside of the meeting rooms."

Everyone got up. Peyton waited while Harper slipped her shoes back on. "Should we get some fresh air?" Harper asked.

Peyton nodded.

They bumped into Ronnie on their way out. "I can't believe I missed the whole segment. I felt terrible abandoning you gals. My stomach went nuts again."

"That's awful," Peyton said. "There are refreshments. Do you want some water or tea maybe?"

"Not yet. I'm not sure if I'm a hundred percent," Ronnie said.

"Fresh air might help," Harper said.

"Yeah. And you can fill me in on what I missed."

Peyton and Harper shot each other looks.

"That bad?" Ronnie asked.

Harper exhaled.

Peyton turned to Ronnie and said, "We have our work cut out for us."

*   *   *

Upon returning to the Japanese garden room, everyone sat exactly as they had before.

"Shall we pick up where we left off?" Liev asked.

"We weren't getting anywhere," Harper said.

"Debate can take time," Ariana said.

Liev nodded. "You must fight. You can't be weak."

"I know I missed a lot of the session and I'm real sorry but I have to respectfully disagree there, Liev. It sounds like we weren't getting anywhere. It should be a conversation, not an argument," Ronnie said.

"The question itself is important. Perhaps we should not take it for granted. Let's return to it. Let's analyze the wording," Ariana suggested.

"We should pick up the debate where we left it," Liev insisted.

Dietrich put his hand up. "May I say something?"

"Go ahead," Milton said, shocking everyone with his first contribution to the discussion.

Dietrich cleared his throat. "I do not intend to be, uh . . ."

"It's okay, say whatever you want," Harper encouraged.

"It's just that we're wasting valuable time," he said.

"Yes, I agree," Liev pronounced.

"Let him finish," Ronnie said.

Liev shook his head, clearly annoyed.

Dietrich fidgeted with his glasses before continuing, "The question is philosophical."

"Oh brother," Liev muttered.

Everyone else groaned.

"Please, if you would just listen for a moment. Even you, Liev, when you first heard it you did not think it was scientific."

"I gave it more thought," he responded.

"Just let Dietrich say his piece," Ronnie interjected.

"It's a philosophical question and if we approach it that way we will be able to work through it. I can facilitate this. Philosophy takes great study and training. People can't just do it, which perhaps is why you resist. I understand, and . . ."

"I'd like to ask you something, Dietrich," Harper said.

He looked nervous. "Yes, please go ahead."

"What do you think when you see a Jackson Pollock painting?"

"I don't understand how . . ."

"Answer honestly. What's your first thought when you see Pollock's masterpiece 'One'?"

He paused for a moment before saying, "To be honest, that I could have made it."

"But you didn't," she said.

"I don't understand your point," he replied.

"You think anyone can make art. It takes less skill than what you do."

Dietrich looked increasingly uneasy.

"When you look at a Pollock you have no idea what you're seeing. Else you wouldn't think you could have made it."

There was silence.

Moments later Liev loudly stated, "We are off track. We're wasting time. Let's get back to it. I will explain again why the question is scientific."

Everyone sat silently as Liev took control of the conversation. Ronnie furrowed her brow and Harper closed her eyes. Peyton berated herself for not speaking up when she had the chance. She picked up her notebook and pen, to refocus on her role as scribe.

✳   ✳   ✳

"I should have been more vocal," Peyton said, taking a forkful of quiche.

"It's just so frustrating," Ronnie said.

"Still queasy, Ronnie? Can I get you a little lunch?" Harper asked.

"Thanks, but I'm covered. Juliette's taking care of me. The kitchen is fixing me a couple of soft-boiled eggs. I don't want to push it."

"I can't believe half the day is gone and we haven't accomplished anything. My hand hurts from taking notes, but they're worthless," Peyton said, flipping through her notebook.

"We got stuck with some megalomaniacs. They're dominating everything," Ronnie said.

"The energy needs to shift," Harper said.

"We're in a rut for sure," Ronnie concurred, as Juliette served her eggs.

"We've got a difficult group," Peyton said. *Figures that would be my luck.*

"Oh, look. Dietrich is leaving the dining hall alone. I feel a bit badly. Afraid I hurt his feelings," Harper said with a wince.

"He's almost as bad as Liev! His way or the highway," Ronnie exclaimed.

"No, I don't think so. Perhaps he's a tad awkward. His affect is kinder," Harper said.

Peyton shrugged, preoccupied with her own anxiety.

"I'm gonna see if I can catch him. Reach out before the next session starts," Harper said, getting up from the table.

✳   ✳   ✳

Dietrich rested his head on his hand. *How am I going to get through to them? Everything I say is misunderstood. Perhaps I shouldn't have spoken when I did.* Lost in thought, he was startled when a sweet voice said, "Hi, there."

He was about to stand up when Harper put her hand on his shoulder. "I don't want to disturb you. May I join you for a bit?"

His eyes widened. "Ah, yes, of course," he said, sliding down on the wrought iron bench.

"Thanks," she said, taking a seat. "Wow! Gorgeous view."

"Oh, uh yes," he stammered, turning his attention forward to the sea and mountains. In truth, he had hardly noticed.

"Perhaps I'll see more of this country after the seminar," she said.

"Do you have plans to extend your trip?"

"Sort of. I'm not sure really where I'll go. Figured I'd travel around Europe a bit. Maybe visit friends in the States."

"You can leave your dance studio indefinitely?" he asked.

"Got a friend running it till I return."

"But you have no itinerary, no reservations, not even a departure date?" he queried.

"Nope. Winging it," she said.

"I've never done anything like that," he said.

"Maybe you should," she replied.

They sat silently looking at the view before Harper continued, "I hope you don't mind. I followed you out."

He tried to mask his surprise.

"I didn't see you out front. Bumped into Diego and he said you walked around back. I can see why. Magnificent, isn't it?" she asked, inhaling deeply.

"Yes. It's quite special," he said, staring at Harper.

For a moment they sat, absorbing the beauty around them. Mustering his courage, Dietrich eventually said, "You were looking for me?"

"Oh, yeah. Just wanted to make sure there were no hard feelings. I didn't mean to pick on you. It was a message to the group really."

"That's perfectly okay. These things happen in debate," he replied.

She smiled. "It needn't be a debate."

He nodded.

"You know, we could be friends. Doesn't matter that we don't see eye to eye," she said.

"I would like that very much," he replied.

"But you can't think I'm a flake, if we're to be friends," she said, smiling coyly.

"I would never, I . . ."

"It's okay. Now that we're friends it's a fresh start," she said, twitching her nose and contorting her face.

He laughed. "Yes, okay. A fresh start."

They sat for another moment before Harper said, "Gee, it's a bit cold. I'm not dressed warmly enough. Better head back in."

"May I ask you one thing first? I'm genuinely curious," Dietrich said.

"Sure."

"When you see one of those Jackson Pollock splatter paintings, have you never thought you could make it too?"

She smirked. "No. Not for a minute. See you inside," she said, patting his arm.

Watching her trot off, Dietrich had one thought: *she's nothing like I expected.*

*   *   *

Notwithstanding the ticking clock, full bellies were not enough to shift the group's focus. The segment after lunch was disastrous. Heels dug in deep. Liev continued to steer the conversation with Ariana's help. Dietrich fought to be heard. Harper tried to interject, this time with more help from Peyton, but it amounted to a Ping-Pong match. Milton sat watching it all. Ronnie quickly ran out, ill again, and missed the entire session.

At designated tea time all of the groups convened in the lounge, a sunshine-filled room with marble floors and white furniture. They were encouraged to socialize before the last official segment of the day.

Ronnie caught up with Peyton and Harper at the tea. "You don't look good," Peyton said.

"I feel worse. Sick as a dog. I think the rough part passed, though. I can't believe how much I missed."

"You hardly missed a thing," Peyton said.

"Still nowhere?"

Peyton nodded. "I'm really worried our group is doomed. What do you think will happen if I can't complete the report?"

"Don't worry," Ronnie said. "There's plenty of time."

"Yeah, Peyton. Relax. You can only do so much," Harper added.

"I have an idea," Ronnie said. "Let's go talk to people in other groups, see how they're doing. Maybe we can get some tips."

"Good idea," Harper said.

Peyton felt anxious. *I don't want to separate. Mingling is the worst. I always feel awkward.*

"Let's grab a cup of tea and go chat with other folks," Ronnie said.

Peyton decided there was no choice but to push past her fear. The women agreed and soon were each enmeshed in conversations with participants from other groups. When the chime alerted them the final formal session of the day was about to begin, they reconvened.

"Well, gals, for better or worse, we're all in the same boat. I talked to the physicist and two literature professors we met yesterday. Their group is deadlocked in battle too," Ronnie said.

"Yeah, the two musicians I chatted with said the same thing about each of their groups," Harper said.

"The women I spoke with said their group gets along pretty well but they're nowhere with the question. They're trying something new in the next session," Peyton said.

"What are they trying?" Ronnie asked.

"They have some kind of activity or game planned. Something creative, but I didn't get the details," Peyton replied.

"Let's all brainstorm on the way over," Ronnie said.

"I think I should suggest interpretive dance. You know, as a way to get comfortable," Harper said.

"Do you really?" Ronnie asked, dubious.

"Not really. But I'd love to see Liev's face," she said.

They laughed all the way back to the Japanese garden room.

* * *

"Let's shake it up," Harper suggested.

"How so?" Ariana asked.

"Well, for starters, let's all swap seats. Reconfigure the energy."

Liev couldn't hide his irritation, but he stood up, prompting everyone else to do the same.

Once reseated, Ariana asked, "Now what? How should we proceed?"

"I have a suggestion," Ronnie said, holding her hand out.

"You have the floor," Ariana said.

"I think we might have gone about this wrong. Instead of attacking the question head on, maybe we need to loosen up, get to know each other and how we think, and free-flow it more."

"That's a good idea," Peyton said, holding her breath, waiting to see how others would respond.

"What do you suggest?" Dietrich asked.

"How about a game?" Ronnie responded.

"What does that have to do with our task?" Liev queried.

"Maybe it will help us communicate. Maybe it will spark new ideas. Maybe it won't help at all, but we're not getting anywhere so I don't see how much it can hurt," Ronnie replied.

"I agree, we need to try something new," Peyton said.

"Yeah. Could be fun," Harper added.

"I'm certain they did not bring us here for fun, but I'll participate if everyone agrees," Liev said.

"Let's try it," Milton said, sealing the deal.

"Great," Ronnie said. "Anyone have any ideas for a game? It could be anything."

They contemplated for a moment before Milton asked, "Any kind of game?"

"Sure," Ronnie said.

"Well, my grandkids get bored at family dinners so we play something they call the category game."

"How do you play?" Harper asked.

"Someone picks a category. It could be anything, like ice cream, dogs, brands of cars, and then you go around in a circle and each person says a type of the category. You're out when it's your turn and you can't think of anything. There's one person left at the end."

"Sounds great," Ronnie said. "Milton, since you came up with it, why don't you pick the first category and get us started."

Milton picked "fruits." It began simply with apples, bananas, pears, and so forth. After a few rounds the fruits became more obscure—like starfruit, kumquats, durian, jackfruit, and rambutan. Dietrich was out first, followed shortly by Ronnie, and then

Ariana. Liev lit up when he shouted "buckthorn berries," crediting his travels for exposing him to the little orange bursts of vitamins. Harper and Milton seemed unstoppable, each with their interest in gardening on full display. When Milton called out the often mistakenly categorized "tomatoes," Harper countered with "avocados," to which Milton rebuffed "pumpkins" next time it was his turn. But Peyton was the dark horse. In the end, to everyone's surprise, she won with "oranges." While they had wracked their brains coming up with exotic fruits, they had forgotten the humble orange. Peyton noticed this early on when other commonplace fruits had been used. She held onto it.

As everyone applauded Peyton's win, Ariana asked, "How many of us had orange juice this morning?"

Five of them raised their hands.

"Interesting," she said.

"Does Peyton select the next category?" Liev asked.

"That's how it's done," Milton replied.

"Oh, okay," Peyton said. "Give me a second." *Vegetables, candy, no, I shouldn't do food again.* "Uh, how about shapes? I'll start with square."

Others followed with circle, triangle, rectangle, and so forth. Once they reached octagon, ellipse, and trapezoid, Peyton and Milton were out. Ariana forfeited when she had to excuse herself to make a phone call. It soon became a lightning round as the remaining four blurted out answers the second it was their turn.

"Stars," Harper said.

Dietrich smiled. "Cylinders."

"Cones," Ronnie said.

"Parabolas," Liev said.

"Lines," Harper said.

"Is a line technically a shape? Is it not shapeless?" Dietrich asked.

"It's a shape with two vertices. It is an acceptable answer," Liev said.

"I see. Okay, I say planes," Dietrich said.

"Oooh, uh. . . . Hmm . . . Gosh I can't believe I can't think of anything. Well I guess I'm out," Ronnie said.

"Points," Liev said.

"Dots," Harper countered.

"Now I must protest," Liev said. "This is not a shape, and if it is, it's the same as a point, which is the proper name."

"I beg to differ. A dot is its own thing. There aren't synonyms for circle or square. Chill out about it," Harper said casually.

Peyton saw a small vein in Liev's forehead start to pulse as his face reddened. She tried to intervene before he exploded. "I think a dot should count. How about you keep going?"

Liev winced.

"It is my turn, yes?" Dietrich asked.

"Yeah, go ahead," Ronnie said.

"Uh, actually I cannot think of anything. I'm out."

"Cyclic polygon," Liev said.

"Never heard of that," Harper said.

"It's a polygonal shape in geometry that you can make a circle around," he replied.

"Interesting. I wasn't challenging you. Just curious," Harper said.

"Do you have a shape or are you out?" Liev asked.

"Squiggle," Harper said.

Liev threw his head in his hands. "That's not a shape," he insisted.

"Why not?" Ronnie asked.

"Sounds like a shape to me," Peyton said. "What do you think, Dietrich?"

"Oh, uh . . ."

"It's not a shape! And if it is, it's the same as a line that you said earlier," Liev exclaimed.

"Well, I think it's different," Harper said. "If it is a version of a line, shouldn't the same rule apply to you?"

"What do you mean?" Liev asked, visibly agitated.

"You said that cyclic thing is a polygonal shape that you can draw a circle around."

"So?" he asked.

"Earlier I said stars. They're cyclic polygons too, right? Wouldn't that mean when you said cyclic it doesn't count? Then I would have won before squiggle."

"She has a point. And someone said squares, triangles, and some others. They are cyclic too," Dietrich added.

Liev looked dumbfounded. "It is not the same. You can't say it after the fact, anyway. Squiggle is not a shape. What's next, a doodle? A splotch?"

"Oh, I love those," Harper said.

"Splotch is a great shape. Very creative," Ronnie said.

Liev shook his head. "I give up."

After a few moments passed they decided to return their focus to the question. Ariana rejoined the group. They remained at odds and ended the day stymied.

Chapter 5

*   *   *

Peyton flipped through her notebook. *Well, I hardly see the point. A whole day of talking amounted to nothing,* she thought as she began transcribing her notes. After recording as much of the day's dialogue as possible, down to the tiniest crumb, she stared at the screen. *A whole lot of nothing. I guess I should add my impressions. It seems futile. How many times can I say we're deadlocked? Or that Liev is a jerk? If only there had been a glimmer of something useful.*

Desperate for a respite, she looked out the window to the sea sprawling before her. It was calming. After glancing at the clock she realized she only had ten minutes before dinner. Afraid of being no closer to writing the final report, she decided to do one more quick read through. *Focus on what you see this time, not how you feel about them,* she told herself. *Hmm . . . that's interesting. Ariana made three points that, well, I don't know, they might have taken us somewhere. She was interrupted by Liev each time. Figures. So I guess we'll never know.* Peyton highlighted the three sentences in her notes.

Ariana said everyone responded to the question based on their field of study.

Ariana suggested we analyze the wording of the question itself.

Ariana noted nobody said "orange" even though the majority drank orange juice earlier.

49

Hmm. I'm probably grasping at straws. Today was horrendous. I'd like to try to get to know Ariana better though. Maybe I misjudged her. We failed but at least she made smart observations. I wonder how things would have gone had we taken her comments more seriously. Skimming her scant notes from the prior day in which she noted being unsure of Ariana, she now determined Ariana was an asset, even if they didn't see eye to eye. *Oh crap, I'm late for dinner!*

*   *   *

Peyton arrived at the dining hall to see her group spread among the crowd. With the exception of Ronnie and Milton, who were sitting together, each member of her group was sitting at a table with people from other groups. Surprised to see Liev and Ariana at separate tables, and Harper at a table in the corner with a bunch of artists, she headed straight to Ronnie, who had saved her a seat.

"Hey there, I was wondering where you were," Ronnie said.

"I lost track of time transcribing my notes. Why isn't Harper sitting with us?"

"Don't know. I think after today maybe she needed a break, you know, be around some new energy. But the bigger news may be Liev and Ariana. They're not sitting together for the first time since we arrived."

"Yeah, I noticed," Peyton replied.

"I was thinking, we should try to hang out with Ariana during the day trip tomorrow. Liev is impossible but if we became friendlier with Ariana maybe we could all work together more effectively."

"That's so strange. When I was typing my notes I had the same thought. You know she made good points today. Like the orange and orange juice comment."

"People rarely see what's right in front of them," Milton said.

"Uh yeah, that's true," Peyton said.

He shrugged and took a bite of mashed potatoes.

"Go grab some chow and we can strategize while you eat," Ronnie said.

"Can I get you anything? How's your stomach?"

"I'm feeling pretty good, considering. But I'm takin' it real easy. Juliette is getting me some white rice and a small piece of poached fish."

"Okay. I'll be right back," Peyton said.

"Get the ham. The ham is delicious," Milton said.

Peyton smiled. "Ham it is."

*　　*　　*

As they finished their desserts, Diego made an announcement.

"Tonight we have something special planned. We have asked several participants to share their artistic and scholarly work in short presentations. It will be a great privilege to learn more about our esteemed colleagues. Please join us in the music hall. You may bring your wine, tea, and coffee."

"Well, this should be interesting. There are so many talented people here," Ronnie said.

"Yeah, I wonder who will be presenting," Peyton said.

People started getting up. Milton took his last bite of chocolate cake before the three of them headed out.

The music hall was set up with rows of chairs. At the front, there was a podium with a piano on the left and a projector and screen on the right.

"I think I should sit on an aisle," Ronnie said. "You know, just in case."

"Sure," Peyton said, taking the seat next to the aisle, in one of the back rows.

People continued to file in, filling the seats. As everyone rustled about in anticipation, Ms. Goodright popped up from a seat in the front row and took to the podium.

"Good evening. We hope your time has been productive. We know that you have been working diligently and must be looking forward to your excursions tomorrow. The forecast is for clear skies and sunshine. As you know, it can get chilly. I suggest you bring a coat. Wear comfortable shoes for your outdoor adventure. There will be many picture-taking opportunities. Do bring your camera or phone. If you need a disposable camera, please let your driver know, they will have several on hand. The vans will be leaving straight away after breakfast. Are there any questions?"

Someone asked, "Should we discuss the question as we sight-see? Is it a working day?"

"That is entirely up to you. We only ask that you have your response by the time the seminar concludes."

Peyton gave Ronnie a sideways look, clearly nervous about the question.

"Now, on to tonight's programming. Curating the participant list for this seminar was a great joy. Your insights, innovations, and achievements boggle the mind. Given the nature of our focused work in small groups, you may not have the opportunity to learn about what each of your colleagues does. That's a shame. So we have invited a few of you to share your work with the larger group. Tonight we will be treated to a presentation on the neuroscience of learning and creativity, a poetry reading, and a musical performance. Please enjoy."

Everyone clapped as Liev headed to the podium with Ariana by his side. Liev explained how neuroscience had historically understood the way people process information. He then proceeded to detail his competing theory about how the human brain processes new information, grounded in decades of research. He broke his theory down into bite-size pieces, using examples anyone could relate to. It was fascinating. He was an impassioned and commanding speaker. It was also clear that he had challenged the common wisdom in the field, turning it on its head and forcing people to think in new ways. Peyton found herself hanging on his every word. At one point, Ronnie flashed Peyton a raised eyebrow. Even she was impressed.

As he finished his presentation, Liev said that Ariana had taken his theory and applied it to the study of creative works. Ariana used MRI scans and other technologies to study how the human brain processes literary works. As she went to the projector, Diego dimmed the lights. Soon there were scans from studies showing people's brains as they consumed poetry. Scans of the same people were taken at multiple times to show the impact of new poetry versus that with which they were familiar. There were also scans of people reading newspapers and other non-literary work. They concluded their presentation to thunderous applause.

"Gee, I hate to admit it, but that was really interesting," Ronnie whispered to Peyton.

She nodded. *It was,* she thought. *They're quite brilliant. Innovative too. Liev is so close-minded with us, but he's courageous in his own work.*

Next a literature professor from Namibia read her poetry and an Austrian classical pianist treated them to a half-hour performance. All the while, Peyton couldn't stop thinking about Liev's presentation, wondering if there was a way they could work together.

✳   ✳   ✳

As people started making their way down to the pub, Peyton spotted Diego in the front of the room.

"Ronnie, I have an idea and I want to ask Diego something. I'll meet you down there."

"Sure thing," Ronnie replied.

Peyton wiggled her way through the crowd.

"Diego, I was wondering if you might be able to help me with something."

"Please, how can I be of assistance?"

"Is it possible to get a special bottle of red wine? Something that would be impressive to a connoisseur? Someone in my group loves fine wines and I thought, well, I thought . . ."

"Yes, I know where we have just the thing. I will bring it to the pub."

"Thank you."

Peyton walked toward the staircase when she noticed Harper near the piano.

"Are you coming to the pub?" Peyton asked.

"Oh, hey there. Yeah, I'll be down in a bit."

Peyton smiled and headed downstairs.

Harper sat down at the piano bench and ran her fingers along the keys. She placed her hands on the keys as if about to play, and held them there.

"Are you going to play something?" Dietrich asked.

"Oh, goodness. Didn't see you there," she said.

"I'm sorry. I didn't mean to startle you."

"Looks like we're the only ones left in here," she said.

"Yes, I was going to the pub like the others when . . ."

"Come, have a seat," she said, sliding down the bench.

"Oh, I . . ."

"Come on," she said.

Dietrich sat down.

"What did you think of the presentations?" he asked.

"Quite interesting. Liev is at his best talking about his work," she replied.

"Ah, yes. He was in his element," Dietrich concurred.

"The poetry was sublime. Her use of metaphors. Wow. You must have loved the pianist," she said.

He smiled. "Yes. He was excellent. The second piece he played is one of my favorites."

"I know you said you don't play any instruments, but perhaps you had piano lessons as a kid?"

He laughed. "Actually, I did. Not for long, though."

"Well, here. Put your hand like this," she said taking his hand and placing his fingers on the keys. "I can play a smidge, and you can help."

"Oh, I don't think I could," he said, putting his arms by his side.

"Sure you can. No one's here. What's the worst that could happen?" she said.

"Well, all right," he said, placing his hand back on the keys.

"Here, you press like this. Just keep it up."

She started playing, with Dietrich doing his part. A cheerful song soon filled the room. Both smiled as they played. After a couple of minutes, Dietrich became distracted looking at Harper and made a mistake. He immediately stopped playing.

"Oh, you didn't have to stop," Harper said.

"Sorry," he said.

"That's okay. It was fun, right?" she said.

"Yes. That song reminded me of something from my childhood."

"I play it for the kids in my class sometimes. I don't even know what it is really. Was your whole family musical?"

"My mother played the piano, as a hobby. She stopped after . . ."

"After what?" Harper asked.

"I had a brother. A twin brother. He died when we were young. The music stopped after that. I never thought about it before actually."

Harper's eyes became watery. She put her hand on Dietrich's arm. "I'm terribly sorry. That must have been enormously difficult."

"Thank you. I didn't mean to make you melancholy."

"You didn't," she said.

Just then Diego walked in.

"Oh, hello. I'm sorry to disturb you. I'm bringing this to Peyton," he said, holding up a wine bottle.

"We're heading down there. Shall we bring it for you?" Harper asked.

"Thank you," he said, handing her the wine. "Good night."

"Shall we join the others?" Harper asked.

Dietrich nodded.

* * *

"Over here," Peyton called, waving to Harper and Dietrich.

"Diego asked me to give you this," Harper said, handing Peyton the bottle of wine.

"Thanks," Peyton said. She rubbed her hand along the bottle, inspecting the label.

"Are you going to crack it open?" Ronnie asked.

"It's not for me."

"It's a bit jollier in here tonight, isn't it?" Harper said, looking around at people engaged in spirited conversations.

"Everyone loved the presentations. Gave us all lots to talk about, I guess. I think it also made folks more comfortable or redirected the energy from the day," Ronnie said.

It's more than that. It's like the people here are surprising us with how special they are, Peyton thought. "Tonight I couldn't help but think everyone here is a like a superhero and they've only started revealing their magical powers," Peyton said.

"Well put. Now let's see if we can get them to use their powers for good," Ronnie said.

"I'm gonna get a drink. Anyone need anything?" Harper asked.

"I'll take a beer, please," Dietrich said.

Harper smiled and traipsed over to the bar.

"So, where were you guys?" Ronnie asked.

"Oh, uh just tinkering on the piano a bit," Dietrich said.

Harper returned and the group carried on chatting for nearly an hour. All the while Peyton was trying to summon the courage to take the bottle of wine to Liev. She thought it might be a way of complimenting him for his research and, more importantly, extending an olive branch. Eventually she got up, wine in hand, and walked over to the entryway to the game room. A large group, including Liev, had been in there all night. She peered into the room. People were drinking, playing games, and chatting. Liev was standing in the far corner talking with a couple of men. *Go on, Peyton. Just walk over and tell him his presentation was great. Tell him his work is fascinating. Then give him the wine. No, offer to share the wine. No, say you had Diego get this from their collection and ask him if it's something he's familiar with. Oh just walk over and say you wanted to compliment him on his presentation and take it from there.* The longer she stood, the more her anxiety rose. *What's wrong with you? You're an adult. Just go over and offer the wine. He does look engaged in conversation already, though. And he has a drink in his hand. It's probably not the right time. I should have done it before he was drinking all night. I missed the moment.*

Someone leaving the game room smiled at Peyton while passing by, making her feel conspicuous. *It's not the right time. I'll save it. Maybe after touring Iceland together it will be easier.*

Peyton started walking to her room, wine in hand, thinking about the day to come. *I hope tomorrow is amazing. Tectonic plates, geysers, waterfalls, and who knows what else. Even the landscape between here and the airport was extraordinary. Like being on another planet. I can't even imagine what tomorrow will bring. I hope I can sleep tonight.* By the time Peyton reached her room she felt one thing above all else: possibility.

Chapter 6

*　　*　　*

Liev's alarm sounded at five o'clock in the morning. Without hesitation, he tapped it off and leapt out of bed. He turned on the radio, preset to the news, and proceeded with his daily exercise. Over the next hour he plowed through a grueling routine until drenched in sweat. As he lathered up in the shower, he began thinking about an article he was writing at the invitation of the editor of an elite journal. *Perhaps I should move the discussion of Martin's theory to an endnote. Readers should be familiar. It's a waste of space. Clutters my point. I should emphasize my theory alone. Yes, I shall move it. It's a special issue and I was asked to write the lead commentary. My work should be primary.* Immersed in thought, he uncharacteristically lost track of time, taking a slightly longer shower than usual, which he realized upon emerging to a steam-filled room. He wrapped a towel around his waist and used his palm to wipe the mirror. He slathered shaving cream on his face and began shaving when another thought sprung to mind. *I should just delete it altogether. If readers do not know the theory, they will not truly understand my work anyway. I shouldn't waste time, holding their hands and spoon-feeding them. They have no business in the deep end. Yes, I shall delete it.* He stared at his reflection proudly, grinning when he carelessly nicked himself on the chin. "Ah, damn," he said. He finished shaving, flushing cold water over his face several times, but the small cut continued to bleed. He covered it with a small piece of toilet paper.

There was a knock on the door. *Right on time.* "Hang on a minute, please," he called, quickly buttoning his shirt. He opened the door to find Diego holding a silver tray with a double espresso, bottle of water, and slice of toast.

"Good morning, Professor," Diego said.

"Good morning, Diego. Thank you," Liev said, taking the tray.

After placing the tray on his desk, he gulped down the espresso, flipped his laptop on, and spent the next hour and a half working on the article, until it was finished. Revisiting his previous thoughts, in the end he included Martin's theory as an endnote, assuming readers would be too lazy to read it on their own and wanting to head off reviewers who might critique him for the omission, as if it were an oversight. *Today's goal met, I can send this off to the journal.* Frustrated at constantly being forced to placate people who didn't grasp his work, he made a show of power by addressing the journal editor by his first name but signing the email with his full title.

At eight o'clock he ate his toast, opened the desk drawer, and removed his pill organizer. He popped open the day's compartment, releasing a handful of pills. One pill dropped to the floor, forcing him onto his hands and knees searching for it. The little blood-soaked piece of toilet paper fell off his chin and to the ground. He sighed, demoralized by the hardest truth of all, his own mortality. When he found the renegade pill, he swallowed it and the others one by one. *Damn, I hate those. You'd think someone would come up with a better delivery system,* he thought, trying to clear the back of his throat from the scratchy trace the large pills left. He chugged the rest of his water, grabbed his jacket, and left for breakfast.

＊　　＊　　＊

Peyton arrived at the dining hall with her arms full, carrying a winter coat, as well as a tote bag packed with a scarf, winter hat, baseball hat, gloves, sunglasses, sweatshirt, tissues, hand sanitizer, notebook, pen, and other miscellaneous items. Given the unpredictable climate, she wanted to be prepared for anything. She immediately spotted her friends and walked over to join them.

"Gee whiz, Peyton, you're a regular old packhorse, huh?" Ronnie said.

"Yeah, I guess," Peyton replied, feeling self-conscious.

"I love that you're prepared! I may hit you up for something," Ronnie said.

Peyton smiled.

"Smart. I always go light. Wind up cold or wet," Harper said.

Dietrich looked quizzically at Harper.

"Yes?" she asked.

"Oh, I . . . I guess I was wondering where you went that you'd end up wet."

Harper giggled.

Peyton placed her belongings on an empty chair. "I'm going to the buffet, does anyone need anything?"

"Oh, today they're offering a choice of the buffet or a bagged breakfast for the car," Ronnie said.

"What are you having?" Peyton asked.

"Bringing something for the car. But I'll go up with you if you want," Ronnie said.

Peyton nodded, and they both headed to the buffet.

Peyton stopped at the beginning of the buffet, vacillating between taking a bowl or a plate. Torn between oatmeal and one of the glistening pastries that had been tempting her at every meal, she stood still, playing a mental Ping-Pong match.

"Oh, go for it. You only live once," Ronnie said, observing her indecision.

Peyton smiled, took a plate and selected an open-face croissant filled with almond cream and apricots. She also put a scoop of fresh berries on her plate, rationalizing the addition made her meal healthier.

"I always agonize about these things," she confessed.

"I hear ya. Sometimes I think I'm lucky I can't eat that stuff," Ronnie said. "Hey, let's try out the cappuccino machine. Because I'm getting a bagged meal for the ride, I need a big ole drink to tide me over."

"Sure," Peyton said, too embarrassed to admit she wanted to try it the day before but was afraid it would be difficult to figure out, with the pressure of others waiting to use it.

Ronnie selected a large cappuccino cup, placed it on the machine, and hit the latte button. The machine started to gurgle, letting off steam, as her hot drink dripped into her cup. "So, you excited for today?" she asked.

Peyton nodded. "Iceland has been on my fantasy travel list for ages. You know, the dream list in your mind that you're probably never going to make it to."

"Oh yeah?" Ronnie asked.

"Uh huh. I just never felt comfortable traveling alone to a foreign country, but it's been on my wish list for a long time. I've read a few travel books about Iceland. I'd love to see the glaciers someday."

"I bet they're spectacular," Ronnie said, retrieving her latte.

Peyton placed a cup on the machine and pressed the cappuccino button. "Yeah, maybe someday I'll make it there. I actually even looked at extending this trip to join a tour group visiting one of the major glaciers, but . . ."

"You should have done it. Maybe it's not too late. You're on summer break, right?"

Peyton shook her head. "Yeah, but if you only knew how much I'm pushing past my comfort zone already. I'm not very, um, daring. Besides, we'll see some amazing stuff today. Are you excited?"

"You bet I am! It's gonna be great!" Ronnie exclaimed. "I told you, I'm an explorer at heart. I've always wanted to see the tectonic plates. I'm planning to take loads of pictures. I'm sure I'll be inspired for when I'm back in my studio. It'll be good to get out of here for a while and get into nature."

Peyton smiled.

"Your drink is ready. Let's head back."

Peyton took her cup. As they walked back she noticed Liev stride into the dining hall, exuding unabashed confidence. She found herself at once repelled and envious.

Chapter 7

✳   ✳   ✳

All of the groups stood outside waiting to be directed to their vans. Harper rubbed her arms. "It's gorgeous but a bit brisk, eh?"

"Will you be warm enough just wearing a sweater and jeans?" Dietrich asked.

"I'll be fine. I've got my good hiking boots at least," she said, kicking her foot up. "It'll warm up some, I imagine. The sun is bright. Was colder this morning when I went for a run. Can't believe this is their summer. Nothing like an Aussie summer."

"Do you run every day?" Dietrich asked.

"Trying to while I'm here. Figured I'd take advantage of the grounds. It was quite cold, though. Pushed me to run faster," she said with a giggle.

"Peyton has extra clothes if you get cold today," Ronnie added.

"Oh yeah, of course. If you need something let me know," Peyton said, noticing she was the only one carrying anything larger than a fanny pack.

Diego approached the group with their driver. "Most of you have already met Aldar, he did the airport runs. He is your group's designated driver for your outings this week."

"Please, this way," Aldar said, holding his arm out toward their van.

Milton sat in the front next to Aldar. Liev and Ariana sat in the second row, Ronnie and Peyton in the third, and Dietrich and Harper in the back.

"If one drives directly it's about forty-five minutes to our first stop, Pingvellir National Park, known for the tectonic plates. I am taking a longer, more scenic route. There are two especially beautiful spots in the mountains along the way where I will stop for picture taking. Please enjoy the ride. I'm happy to answer any questions you have."

Peyton looked out the window, admiring Crystal Manor, shimmering in the sunshine. As it became smaller, she remembered the first time she saw it. *That was the start of an adventure. I guess today will be too. I wonder if we'll talk about the question. I hope we do. We're so far behind. I'm the one stuck with the report. I'll be mortified if we don't figure it out. I wonder if they'll bill us for the trip. Oh God, they wouldn't do that, would they? I can't afford it . . .*

"Hey, Aldar, what can you tell us about those purple flowers?" Ronnie asked, interrupting Peyton's stream of consciousness.

"Those are nootka lupine, also called Alaskan lupine. They look right at home here, covering much of our landscape, but they are not indigenous. They were brought here in 1945. You are lucky to visit at this time of year. They only bloom for a short period. Tourists always remark on them. The first pit stop is an excellent place to photograph them."

"I think they're the same flowers they brought to our rooms the day we arrived," Ronnie said.

"Small ones, perhaps. They can grow quite big in nature," Aldar said.

"They were brought in to help with land reclamation and reforestation," Milton said.

"Oh yeah?" Ronnie prodded.

"Yes. To add nitrogen to the soil, among other things," Milton replied.

"Has it worked?" Peyton asked.

"Depends on who you ask," Milton said.

"It's controversial," Aldar added.

"It spread more than they expected. Sheep and goats don't eat the nootka lupine. There's been talk of crossbreeding to make a hybrid animals could graze on, which could solve a couple of problems at once," Milton said.

"You sure know a lot about it," Ronnie said. "I'm impressed."

"I am too," Aldar said. "Perhaps you and I should team up to give tours."

Milton shrugged.

"It's interesting they brought something in, something not indigenous, planted it, didn't predict how far it would spread, and now see it as threatening their ecosystem, if I understand you correctly," Ariana said.

"Yup. You got it," Milton replied.

"Now that they don't like its behavior, their solution is manipulate it, to literally make it more palatable," she continued.

"That's right," Milton said.

"Remarkable," Ariana replied.

The implications of Ariana's remarks intrigued Peyton so much she considered jotting something in her notebook. *I better not,* she thought. *Hopefully I'll remember later.* She looked out the window admiring the soil dark as coffee grounds, forming mounds and mountains, speckled with purple flowers dotted in white. *How strange and magnificent.*

✳   ✳   ✳

Clouds swiftly rolled in. The blue sky, now shades of gray, looked as if it might begin to cry.

"Hey, Aldar. The weather seems to have changed quickly. You think it will rain?" Ronnie asked.

Aldar laughed. "The weather does as she pleases. One never knows. But I think it will pass."

Peyton thought the landscape was even more beautiful in this light. Everywhere she looked there were mountains the color of milk chocolate pudding, with swirls of green and yellow green. The clouds hung, suspended at the tops of the mountains, creating a fuzzy dullness where she imagined either the mountains ended or the sky began. Occasionally sheep lined the road. With endless room to graze, they stuck close to the one winding road. *How odd,* Peyton thought. *I wonder why they do that.* Every time they passed a creek or pond, someone remarked on the beauty.

Aldar pulled the car onto a dirt path, leading to an open plateau amid mountains. "This is the first spot I mentioned," he said, as he parked the car.

"Wow, it's wild!" Ronnie exclaimed.

"I will come around and open the sliding door," Aldar said.

Milton hopped out and stretched his arms as the others filed out. They stood entirely surrounded by a vista of mud-colored mountains covered in nootka lupine.

"Please, feel free to look around and take some pictures if you like. I will stay by the van," Aldar said.

Everyone wandered around, admiring the scenery. Harper asked Dietrich to take a picture of her. Ronnie took dozens of close-up photos of the flowers. Peyton breathed deeply, taking in the indescribable smell of the soil. Wherever she walked, small insects followed, hovering around her face, as the sheep had hovered close to the street. She swatted at them a few times, shaking her head, afraid some took up residence in her hair. Ronnie walked over, as Peyton flung her hands out again.

"The bugs getting you?" Ronnie asked.

"They seem to love flying around my face. I hope they don't bite. The one thing I didn't bring was insect repellent," she lamented.

"I'm not sure what they are. I'll ask for you when we go back," Ronnie said.

Peyton smiled. Somehow Ronnie was like a lifelong best friend, one who knew she was too shy to ask herself.

"Check out these pictures," Ronnie said, scrolling through the gallery in her phone. "I zoomed in as closely as I could to the dots on the flowers, without making 'em blurry. I already have an idea brewing. I'm gonna blow these up when I get back home."

"That's really cool," Peyton said.

"I want to capture everything we see, chronologically, for an installation."

"I'm fascinated with how artists see things. I know when we both look at the flowers, I'm not seeing what you're seeing," Peyton said.

"And I'm not seeing what you're seeing," Ronnie said.

Ariana and Liev passed by, on their way back to the van.

"I think it's time to go," Peyton said.

As they arrived at the van, Aldar asked, "A nice spot, yes?"

"Sure is. But tell me, do the bugs flying around bite?" Ronnie asked.

"No, they merely annoy people. They do not bite," he replied.

"You're good to go," Ronnie said to Peyton as she hopped into the van. Peyton smiled, relieved by the news and grateful for her friend.

✳   ✳   ✳

Deitrich adjusted his glasses and said, "This is a beautiful car ride."

"Look out my side," Harper said softly. "Looks like the surface of Mars or something, eh?"

Dietrich leaned closer as Harper turned her head to face the window and he caught a whiff of her tropical shampoo. "Uh yes, I've never seen terrain like this before."

"Makes me think about how much more there is to see in this world. More than anyone can experience. We get such a small slice, you know?"

"That's why I take advantage of opportunities to give lectures abroad," he replied.

"Something about this place makes me wonder what's beyond earth. Can't help but imagine what things are like at the margins of our galaxy and beyond," she said. "Do you believe there's life on other planets?" she asked, turning back to face him.

"Well it depends on what you mean by life. A plant is a form of life. But I think talk of Martians and all that is hocus pocus. Perhaps you think differently?"

"Do I believe there's life on Mars?" she asked with a giggle. "I believe somewhere out there David Bowie is making music we can no longer hear. But aliens, no, not really. Though I'm open to being wrong."

Dietrich smiled. "So no Martians but maybe some sort of after-life?" he asked.

"Yes, I think so. We're energy. That energy must go somewhere, in some form. You must have given this thought after your brother passed."

Dietrich looked down and adjusted his glasses.

"Oh dear, I'm sorry," Harper said, placing her hand on his.

"Please, don't be sorry. I did think about it, for many years. I've used the tools I have to search for answers but . . ."

"But you end up with more questions," she said.

"Yes, exactly," he said.

"May I ask what your brother was like?"

"Certainly. Uh, well, he was better with people than I am," he said with a chuckle.

"Nonsense. What else?" she asked.

"He was very smart. He excelled in science. Our parents thought he'd become a famous scientist. I'm sure he would have. I never had a mind for it like he did."

"Interesting you became a philosopher," she said.

He furrowed his brow. "Because they are opposites? Yes, we were close friends but quite different."

"No, because they're so similar. You both wanted to make sense out of the world. Order out of chaos really. Just different lenses."

That thought settled in Dietrich's heart and the smell of coconut shampoo lingered in the air. He was about to open his mouth when Harper tapped his shoulder, "Look, look at that mountain," she said, pointing to the horizon.

* * *

As a magnificent lake appeared before them, Liev remarked, "Quite a sight."

Ariana stretched forward for a better view. "That's spectacular, Aldar. Might we have an opportunity to stop?" she asked.

"Yes. This is our next stop. There is a space to pull over down the road," he replied.

"What can you tell us about it?" Ariana asked.

"This is the largest natural lake in Iceland, a rift valley lake. The islands originate from volcanoes."

"So we must be near the tectonic plates," Ronnie said.

"Yes. After this stop we are almost at the park where you will have an hour to walk around," he said.

Mountains surrounded the lake, with islands in the center, each casting a small dark gray shadow. The lake mirrored the sky— silver kissing silver. Clouds hovered just above as if hugging the mountains.

Aldar parked the car at a landing and everyone hopped out, joining a smattering of tourists and artists.

"The color is extraordinary," Peyton said to Ronnie. "It's otherworldly. Like the color of a unicorn or something."

"Yeah, it's real mystical looking in this light. We're actually lucky the weather turned since the water takes on the color of the sky. That's why Monet painted the same spots over and over again, because the light constantly changes. Light changes everything," Ronnie said.

Peyton smiled.

"Come down here," Harper called from ahead.

Everyone stood near each other, clicking away on their camera phones and talking about the spellbinding view. After a few minutes Ronnie said, "I'm gonna grab my food."

"Peyton, would you take a picture of me?" Harper asked.

"Sure," she said, taking her phone.

"Do you want me to take one of you?" Harper asked.

"Oh, I don't think so, well . . . yeah, okay," she said, realizing she'd regret not capturing the moment.

After they took the photos Ronnie rejoined them, holding a sandwich.

"Is it good?" Peyton asked.

"Oh yeah, it's their take on a breakfast sandwich I guess; smoked salmon, cucumber, sliced egg, and dill on g-free bread. They packed it with a small ice bag. I didn't want to eat before the car ride, just in case."

"Do you still feel sick?"

"Nope, but sometimes if it's not out of your system, when you eat it hits you again," she said, taking a bite.

"Got ya," Peyton said, swatting another bug away from her face.

"They sure do like you," Ronnie said.

Peyton sighed. *Just my luck.*

＊　　＊　　＊

Buzzing about the scenery, everyone was chatting away in the van. Even Milton was talking to Aldar. Peyton noticed Ronnie was uncharacteristically quiet and squirming in her seat.

"Are you okay?" Peyton asked.

Ronnie shook her head. "I need a restroom."

"Excuse me, Aldar, how much farther is it?" Peyton asked.

"Only a few minutes," he replied.

"Can you make it?" Peyton whispered to Ronnie.

"I think so," she said, hunched over, holding her stomach, and scrunching her face.

"Aldar, when we arrive is there a restroom nearby?" Peyton asked.

"Yes. I will drop you off in the front. The building with the facilities is to the left, there's a gift shop and café in front, and the path through the park to the right. You will have one hour to sightsee. At the end of the path, there are bridges to the right. I will be parked in the lot down there. If you need me beforehand I will be in the lot where I am dropping you off, to stretch my legs and have a coffee."

"We're almost there, Ronnie. I'll take you to the bathroom if you want," Peyton whispered.

"Thanks, you're a pal," Ronnie said, clenching her stomach.

When they arrived Ronnie flew out of the van. Peyton followed, calling out to the rest, "I'll meet up with you."

They arrived at the restroom to discover a 100-króna charge. Ronnie frantically searched her fanny pack when Peyton calmly handed her the money.

"Thanks," she said, getting in line. "Go meet the others. I'll find you."

"I'll use it too while we're here. I don't mind waiting for you," Peyton said.

"I'll be a while. You should go ahead," Ronnie said.

Peyton agreed.

Harper and Ariana came in and got in the back of the line just as Ronnie dashed into a stall. "Everyone's using the WC first," Harper called.

Peyton nodded. "Ronnie needs some time. She'll meet up with us later."

*   *   *

The group met outside the restrooms, minus Ronnie.

"Shall we get going?" Liev asked.

Everyone nodded, and they started to make their way to the trail. A bridge overlooking the area was to the right of the top of the footpath, so they headed there first. The whole area was teeming with tourists, and it was difficult to stay together. Liev and Ariana were quickly ahead of the pack with Milton casually trailing behind.

Peyton looked down at her feet, shuffling ahead.

"Hey there. You all right?" Harper asked.

"I feel badly for Ronnie," Peyton replied.

"Yeah, she sure is havin' a tough time," Harper said.

"She really wanted to take photographs of this, for an art project. I'm going to do my best to take them for her."

"Good idea," Harper said. "Is that the only thing bothering you?"

"Well, we just got here and already we're not really together," Peyton replied.

"Yeah, everyone's going at their own pace, I suppose," Harper said.

"I'm just worried we won't finish our task in time. I mean, they sent us in our groups so they must expect us to use this time somehow," Peyton said, anxiety tied to each word.

"Yeah, it's early yet. And this spot's a bit crowded. Don't be discouraged. Come on, let's get those photos for Ronnie," Harper said, holding her arms wide open.

Peyton smiled and pulled her phone out of her coat pocket. She held it up, looking at the panoramic view on the screen: rocks, canyons, streams. *This is pretty awesome. I hope Ronnie gets to see it.*

＊　　＊　　＊

The crowd thinned out once they were off the bridge, and they were again a group, minus one. Large rocks piled high on both sides formed walls that led the way.

"I've never seen a landscape like this before," Ariana said.

"A fissure zone is unique. See those rock formations," Liev said pointing. "You will not see something like that except in a rift valley."

"It's magical," Harper said.

"It's scientific," Liev responded. "I can explain the geological significance if it would be beneficial."

Harper laughed. "I understand the geology. But being here, breathing it in, that's not so easily mapped. Except maybe for a poet, eh?"

Liev rolled his eyes at Ariana, clearly confused by what Harper was rattling on about.

"I understand what you mean," Ariana said, turning to Harper. "For me, the scope of it is something you can only feel when you're here, experiencing it," she continued.

Peyton smiled. *I'm really starting to like Ariana.*

As they approached a staircase to the right, Liev asked, "Shall we get a view from up there?"

Everyone said yes except for Peyton, who said she wanted to get more shots of the rock formations and would wait down on the path. That was only partly true. Terrified of heights, she held no desire for an elevated view. Losing her footing and plummeting to her death in a freak accident, forever being branded the "unfortunate American tourist," was high on her list of worries, although she knew it was probably ridiculous.

She began to take random shots of the rocks. *I wonder what Ronnie would want. She took a bunch of close-ups of the flowers. I think she was trying to get different angles. Maybe I should get close-ups.* As Peyton zoomed in she made a splendid discovery: there were faces in the rocks. At first she thought it was a fluke or that she might be imagining it, but as she looked at rock after rock, she saw faces in nearly each one. *That one has a strong nose. That one looks like it's smiling. It even has moss for hair. Wow, those two look like they're having a private conversation. The one on the left has such a mischievous expression, as if the other one just told it a secret.* Enthralled by what she saw, Peyton continued scanning the rocks. *Oh, I love the one with the grimace and moss for his nose and those bushy eyebrows. Crooked teeth! That one is the old man with crooked teeth. I have to capture this all for Ronnie,* she thought as she began clicking away from different angles.

"Hey there," Harper said, startling Peyton.

"Oh, hey. I didn't see you guys come back down," she replied.

"The view was gorgeous," Ariana said. "We can wait a few minutes if you changed your mind."

"Thanks but that's okay. I've been having fun taking pictures of the rocks." She paused, nervous to continue but decided to see how they'd react. "I don't know if you see it, but I see faces in them. See, look at that one," Peyton said, pointing to old man with crooked teeth.

"Um, I'm not sure," Harper said.

"Which one?" Ariana asked.

"Over there," Peyton said.

"Yes, I do see it! How funny," Ariana said.

"Look at the one next to it," Peyton said.

Ariana laughed. "You're right. It's marvelous."

"Look at that one," Harper said.

"Liev, do you see this?" Ariana asked.

Liev inspected the rocks and shook his head.

"What about that one? The crack is where the mouth is," Ariana said.

"Ah, yes. I see," Liev said.

They continued down the path, searching for the unseen. Liev pointed out a couple of bodies in the rock formations he thought Peyton should photograph for Ronnie. Peyton took hundreds of pictures. When they passed tiny yellow and magenta flowers, she stopped to capture them from multiple distances, which she remembered Ronnie had done at the nootka lupine.

The sound of crashing water guided them to a natural waterfall with bright white caps folding themselves into deep turquoise water, clear enough to see granular patterns in the sand on the floor. The beauty spoke for itself, so they added no words. After everyone snapped a few shots they continued down the path. Liev and Milton chatted about the science behind nature. Harper and Dietrich discussed their travel fantasies. Peyton and Ariana meandered behind, taking in the scenery.

Say something to her, Peyton thought. *Now's my chance to get to know her better. It was nice of her to offer to wait if I wanted to go to the higher level. She didn't think I was nuts for pointing out the faces. She's been really friendly. It's not hard to just say something. Oh God, I wish Ronnie was here.*

Ariana looked over and smiled. *It's like she can hear my thoughts. She must think I'm a freak.* "The rock formations are incredible. I've never seen anything like it before," Peyton said.

"I know. We are blessed to be here. I love the expressions you identified. Once you see them you can't stop," Ariana said.

"Yeah, at first I thought it was just in my head," Peyton replied.

"Well, who knows? We see what we think we can see. One person can affect what others think they see," Ariana said.

"That's true," Peyton said.

"But I think they're really there, the faces," Ariana said, smiling.

Everyone continued chatting, and when an hour had passed they made their way to the parking lot. Ronnie was sitting in the van looking like a rag doll.

"I hope you don't mind, I used the hand sanitizer in your tote bag," Ronnie said.

"Of course not," Peyton replied.

"Oh dear, did you get a chance to see anything?" Harper asked.

"Not really. I spent nearly an hour in the restroom. I was afraid to leave and have to get back in line. Aldar was nice enough to wait for me. He drove me down to pick you all up."

"I'm so sorry, Ronnie. Are you feeling better?" Peyton asked.

"I think so. Aldar said our next stop isn't far, and there's a restroom there if I need it. I feel terrible I missed spending this time with all of you."

"There's nothing you can do if you're sick," Liev said.

"We'll have more time together," Harper said.

"Thanks, guys," Ronnie said, leaning her head against the window.

"Ronnie," Peyton whispered.

"Yeah," she said, turning to face her.

"I took these pictures for you. I hope they're alright. I know I don't have your art eye but I tried to get as many details as I could. Here," she said, handing over her phone.

Ronnie smiled. "You're the best. Thank you!"

Ronnie began scrolling through the photos when Peyton asked, "Do you see anything? Anything out of the ordinary in the rocks?"

"Ha. Look at that. The rocks have faces. Just like those paintings at the Manor. I guess that artist was just painting what he saw."

Peyton smiled. *I knew Ronnie would see it. I wonder if she's right, that he was just painting what's there. Or maybe he saw something new. I think he made us see something we wouldn't otherwise, real or not. What's real anyway?*

Chapter 8

*   *   *

They pulled into a parking lot amid a flurry of tourist buses. "There is a large gift shop and restrooms in that building. If you're looking to buy souvenirs, I suggest you stop in before we depart. Please meet me at the van in forty-five minutes and we will go to lunch," Aldar said.

Harper rubbed her arms. "Peyton, can I please borrow a scarf or something? Was a bit chilly at the last stop. It's still overcast."

"Of course," Peyton said, handing her a black cashmere scarf.

They disembarked from the van. As the group crossed the street, they saw steam rising from the ground. The air, thick with the smell of sulfur, nauseated Ronnie immediately.

"Guys, I can't take the odor. I'm gonna go inside," she said.

"Are you sure?" Peyton asked.

Ronnie nodded.

"I feel so badly for you. Do you want me to come with you?" Peyton asked.

"No way. Go check it out. I'll be fine."

Everyone told Ronnie to feel better and waved as she walked away.

"And then there were six," Harper said.

Peyton sighed.

"It's horrible when you suffer from nausea. There is nothing you can do to get your bearings," Liev said.

Peyton caught Harper's eye, both noting Liev's refreshing sympathy.

Dietrich sniffed deeply into his nostrils. "They do smell quite foul," he said matter-of-factly.

"Let's call it what it is, farts on steroids!" Ariana exclaimed.

They all laughed.

"Well come on, let's have a look around," Liev said.

This landscape was in stark contrast to where they had just been. A bumpy terrain of brown dirt, mud, and rocks, with cracks and craters, like the surface of the moon, surrounded by scattered grass patches with little purple, yellow, and white flowers representing life. In the distance beyond the craters there was a splattering of grass, trees, and mountains.

People were drawn to this peculiar place to stand at the edge of the geysers: pools of water, emitting steam that swirled like smoke. Everywhere one looked across this craterous surface, there were spots where steam rose from the ground, Mother Nature letting her emotions seep out. Some geysers were small, just puffs of rising steam. Others were pools of spectacularly bright aqua that Ariana dubbed "technicolor or neon." The largest, famous for its eruptions, attracted a crowd around it.

"Let's see the big one," Liev suggested. They stood, waiting for it to blow.

"We're gonna get wet," Milton said.

"I think it will be some light spray," Liev said.

"I'm going over there," Peyton said. "I don't want to get wet."

"Me too," Ariana said.

"It's just mist," Liev called as they walked away.

Seconds later the geyser blew, drenching Liev, Milton, Dietrich, and Harper.

Harper couldn't stop laughing, twirling around in delight.

"I should have taken my glasses off," Dietrich said.

"I told you," Milton said.

Liev was speechless.

Dietrich held his glasses, looking for a dry spot on his clothing to wipe them.

"Here, give 'em to me," Harper said, extending her hand. "My scarf isn't wet. Lucky I borrowed it."

"Thank you," he said as she returned the glasses, dry.

Harper giggled. "This kind of thing always happens to me."

Dietrich smiled. "Yes, when you mentioned at breakfast you always wind up wet or something I couldn't quite imagine how. Now I see."

The four made their way to Peyton and Ariana, who had enjoyed the eruption from a safe distance.

"I have extra clothes in the van if anyone needs to borrow something," Peyton said.

Just then the sky began to change.

"Look at that, the sun's breaking through," Harper said.

They walked around a little longer. By the time they went to the gift shop the sun was shining brightly and everyone was beginning to dry off and warm up.

"Aldar was right. Things can change quickly," Ariana said, removing her coat.

They can, Peyton thought.

✳   ✳   ✳

As the van approached a small hotel where they were to have lunch, everyone else was looking at trinkets they bought at the geyser gift shop—magnets, postcards, jewelry, and books, while Peyton was deep in thought. *How will we ever make progress answering the question? We saw such beauty today. And everyone's getting along. I wish I could enjoy it more. Ronnie being out of commission is making it harder. Maybe lunch will be our chance to talk, all of us as a group. I wonder if anyone will bring it up.*

"And here we are," Aldar said. The unassuming gray stucco building didn't look like much. "This hotel has a nice lunch spot with gorgeous views. Please go inside. They're expecting you. I'll be at the van when you're ready."

Everyone hopped out and made their way inside. There wasn't a soul in sight, just a small, unwatched reception desk.

"There's a sign, the restaurant is this way," Liev said, heading to the right.

They arrived in an airy, casual dining area, featuring a long wall of glass windows overlooking rolling green hills. The view was again unlike any of the others they had seen. They stood awkwardly, clearing their throats and making other innocuous noises to signal their presence. A rotund woman with honey blonde curls crashed through the swinging kitchen doors.

"Well forgive me. I hope you haven't been waiting long. You're the group from Crystal Manor, yes?"

"Yes," Liev and Dietrich replied in unison.

"Wonderful, I'm Birta. We're putting the final touches on your lunch. Please, go seat yourselves at that large table by the window. Best view in the place," she said before running off.

"How odd we're the only ones here," Peyton said.

"It's late for lunch," Liev said.

"Maybe they closed for our group," Harper mused.

By the time they seated themselves, Birta was rushing over with a pitcher of water.

"What can I get you each to drink? We have soda, juice, wine, beer, coffee, and tea."

Oh, I hope no one orders alcohol, Peyton thought. *They won't want to work.*

"I'll have a beer, please," Dietrich said.

"Me too," Liev said.

"Make it three," Milton said.

"When in Rome," Harper joined in.

Well, maybe it's a good thing. Maybe it will loosen them up, Peyton rationalized before she, Ariana, and Ronnie said they were fine with water.

They sat for a moment enjoying the serene view.

"Looks like it could be a golf course," Harper said. "Wonder if it is."

"I doubt it," Liev said.

Peyton noticed Ronnie was quiet. "You feel okay?" she whispered.

"Yeah. I'm just really disappointed I missed so much."

Birta came bursting through the kitchen doors again, with a man in cook's clothing behind her. They delivered their drinks, a loaf of bread, and a large bowl of salad.

"We prepared a family-style lunch for you. We'll bring the rest out in a minute. I know there are allergy concerns. Fear not, it's all gluten and lactose free. Even the bread."

"That's nice," Peyton said.

Ronnie nodded.

Moments later Birta and the cook returned with roast chicken surrounded by potatoes and root vegetables and a platter of slow-cooked arctic char topped with microgreens.

Dietrich offered to walk around the table with the platter of chicken so everyone could help themselves.

"Lovely they made it family-style," Harper said as she passed the salad.

"Really homey," Ariana added.

The food smelled delicious. Even Ronnie took a chicken thigh and potatoes.

Everyone was enjoying their first few bites when Peyton again began to wonder if anyone would bring up the question. *Doesn't seem like they will. I should say something. But . . .*

Ariana interrupted her thoughts when she said, "This is a great opportunity to break bread together. Perhaps we should use this time to talk about the question."

Peyton looked to see their reactions before jumping in. "I agree. Let's make the most of the time we have together."

"Good idea," Harper said.

"Yes, let's be productive," Liev concurred.

"How should we begin?" Ariana asked.

They sat, the only noise the sound of chewing. A couple of minutes passed before Ronnie said, "Maybe we should tackle it indirectly. Then tomorrow back at the lodge we can take a more direct approach."

Peyton smiled, unable to hide her joy that Ronnie was participating again.

"I had a thought," Harper said.

"Yes, what is it?" Dietrich asked.

"Might be nothing but I'm wondering if it's important they put us in groups of seven. It's not fifty participants, it's forty-nine."

"I noticed the number seven was a part of a larger number on my welcome packet. I think it was seven at least," Peyton said.

Ariana nodded. "The number seven has a rich history. Perhaps if we talk about it we'll stumble on to something."

Everyone seemed to agree.

"Should someone take notes?" Ariana asked before eating a bite of carrots.

"I think we can be informal and let everyone enjoy lunch," Liev said.

Peyton took a small notebook and pen out of her bag. "I don't mind jotting a few things down."

"Maybe we should start by listing the most obvious things that come to mind. Then we can see how it develops," Ariana suggested.

"Sounds good," Ronnie said. "I'm happy to get us going. What first comes to mind for me is the seven continents."

Ariana smiled. "For Americans that's a good example, but there's a cultural element to geography and what is considered a continent. It's not universal."

Hmm. Peyton thought. *That's interesting. We are an international group. Maybe we should talk about that.* But the moment escaped her.

"There are seven seas," Milton said.

"And seven wonders of the world," Harper said. "Oh, and something in music too, uh . . . "

Dietrich smiled. "There are seven distinct notes in the diatonic musical scale," he said.

"Yes!" Harper exclaimed.

"There are seven holes in the human head," Milton said before asking Liev to pass the potatoes.

"That's funny. I never thought of that," Harper said.

"I'm sure there's a good joke in there," Ariana mused.

"Seven is considered a lucky number," Peyton said.

"Yeah, when you roll two dice, seven has the highest probability of coming up," Ronnie said.

"Slot machines pay off with triple sevens," Milton added.

Harper looked at him curiously.

"My wife and I go to Atlantic City sometimes," he said.

Harper smiled. "Do you get saltwater taffy? I loved that stuff as a kid."

"I like the peppermint," Peyton said.

Milton shook his head. "Too chewy. Never touch it."

Ronnie chimed in, "You know, to go in a bit of a different direction if that's okay, one of the first things that I thought of hearing the number seven was popular culture. Maybe it's different in other places, but in American pop culture seven appears a lot in films, books, and so on."

"I think it holds true to some extent," Ariana said. "*Harry Potter* comes to mind. Seven is important in those books. And with the prominence of Hollywood we're probably all exposed to many of the same things, for better or worse."

Dietrich agreed. "I admit I enjoy the James Bond movies, 007."

Harper smiled.

They all continued eating and everyone began listing books and movies from William Shakespeare to Neil Gaiman. After twenty minutes, they had full bellies but were running short on ideas. Birta came to clear the dishes and serve coffee, tea, and a small tray of pastel-colored macaroons.

"May I say something?" Dietrich asked.

"Go ahead," Milton said.

"When I hear the number seven what comes to my mind is religion. Seven is an important number in many religions. Of course the Old Testament says that the world was created in seven days, the seventh being the day of rest."

"Yes," Peyton said. "In Kabbalah it says that because God rested on the seventh day he added a spiritual dimension to the world. Seven is considered a spiritual number."

Liev concurred. "For the record, I don't think any of this seven discussion is relevant but nevertheless Christianity is full of references to seven: deadly sins, gifts from God, sacraments."

Dietrich nodded. "In Revelation, the Seventh Angel will blow the seventh trumpet seven times and a lamb will break open the seven seals to reveal the mystery of God."

"Seven is prominent in other religions, too. I can think of examples in Hinduism, Taoism, and Judaism," Ariana said.

Harper said, "It's not just organized religions. I'm not religious. I've read a lot about New Age spirituality though."

Liev pursed his lips.

Harper continued. "Seven is the path of introspection according to some."

"I think we've taken this as far as we can, talking in circles," Liev said.

"I want to mention one other thing," Harper said. "Seven shows up in mythology too."

Liev rubbed his eyes, visibly losing his patience.

"Tell us more," Ronnie said.

"Atlas had seven daughters. They helped populate the heavens. Zeus turned them into a seven star configuration," Harper said.

"We've reach fantasy at this point. Mythology is nonsense," Liev shrieked.

"Not everyone feels that way. Perhaps you're just a bit closed minded," Harper rebuffed.

"I did not want to say this earlier but if seven is important, it's because of neuroscience," Liev said.

"Well gee, that's a novel conclusion for you!" Ronnie exclaimed.

"It is the truth. There is a neurological basis for humans' preference for seven. We can generally remember seven-digit numbers, not eight. It's quite simple. Our brains are best able to store the number seven. If the number seven is some sort of clue, it is pointing us back to science, as I have said from day one."

Everyone was speechless. Milton picked up his coffee cup and slurped his last sip, breaking the silence.

Birta came over and asked, "Can I get you anything else?"

Peyton shook her head. "I think we're done."

✳   ✳   ✳

"Gullfoss is Europe's most powerful waterfall. It's one of the natural wonders of the world," Aldar said as he parked the van.

"Is it a protected site?" Ariana asked.

"Yes. It is a designated nature reserve," Aldar replied. "When you walk over you will see it is split into upper and lower waterfalls. There's a staircase, and I recommend you venture up to the top to experience every view. You will also notice the color of the water is remarkable and changes in different lighting. The magic of glacial water. Please return to the van when you're done. There's no rush."

Everyone got out and started walking toward the massive crashing waterfall. It wasn't until they were close that they realized a large crevice had been obscured from view and the water was plummeting into a canyon below.

"Wow! It's spectacular," Harper said.

"Awe-inspiring," Ariana said.

Everyone took photographs for a few minutes before Liev said, "Shall we follow the lower path and then head up to the top?"

Peyton looked at the steep staircase off to the left and began to panic. *I can't believe how high it is. I can't go up there,* she thought, but she said nothing. They began following the lower path, toward the thunderous sound of crashing water.

"The mist feels good," Harper said.

Peyton smiled. "The color is beautiful. I've never seen water like this."

"It's because of the sediments in glacial water," Milton said.

"How do you know so much about it?" Harper asked.

"Nature enthusiast. That's my life."

"That's interesting about the sediments," Ronnie said. "Can you tell us more?"

Milton regaled the group with his vast knowledge of different kinds of water all the way to the end of the path.

They were taking pictures when Ariana said, "Seeing how unique the glacial water is makes me think about the glaciers."

"Peyton really wants to visit some of the glaciers," Ronnie said.

Peyton smiled. "Yeah, maybe someday."

Liev put his phone in his pocket and turned to Peyton. "Someday is always in the distance. Someday is dangerous. Be careful of someday."

Peyton felt like he could see right through her. *I can't believe he said that to me, like he knows I'll never get there. He's probably right too.* Unsure of how to respond, she was relieved when Dietrich said, "The glaciers may not exist someday if humans do not make serious changes. I know Icelanders are rightfully concerned."

Ariana nodded. "Exactly what I was thinking," she said. "It's especially sad for people living in more ecologically responsible cultures to be at the mercy of those countries who do not care. We all share this one planet. The many have their fate sealed by the few."

Harper chimed in, "What I don't understand is the CEOs of these companies and the politicians who support them have families too. Don't they worry for their grandchildren's futures?"

"They don't believe in science," Liev said. "They are stuck in their dinosaur mentality."

Ronnie nodded. "It is dinosaur thinking. That dinosaur thinking will be their end. It's gonna eat 'em for lunch one day."

"And all of us too, I fear, if we don't find a new way to think," Ariana said.

Dinosaur thinking. A new way to think. Hmm. Peyton thought before drifting back to Liev's earlier comment. *I wonder why he said that to me about someday. It's like he sees my hesitance. Is he judging me?* Liev's voice broke her stream of consciousness.

"Okay, shall we head back and go to the upper level?" he asked.

Oh no, I really can't go up there. I mean, I kind of want to, but I can't.

*   *   *

A few minutes later they were standing at the base of a precipitous staircase. Peyton looked up with dread. Her heart began to beat faster. *Maybe it's not as high as it seems,* she rationalized. Just as Liev was about to step up, Peyton panicked and blurted out, "I'm gonna wait down here. I don't want to go up there."

Liev turned around and asked, "Why not? What's the problem?"

Harper replied, "She's afraid of heights. Remember?"

"Ah, it's perfectly safe," Liev insisted.

"Our fears aren't always rational," Dietrich said.

I'm so embarrassed. I can't believe this is becoming such a big deal, Peyton thought.

"If you don't feel comfortable, there's no pressure," Ariana said.

Peyton tilted her head. "Thank you. I just . . . I just . . ."

"Hey," Ronnie said, rubbing Peyton's arm. "I'm still pretty low energy. I can stay down here with you."

"Oh, no. You missed so much already. Please go," Peyton said. "I actually sort of want to go too, it's just that I'm worried I'll start up and be too scared. I don't want to get stuck."

The corners of Liev's mouth turned upward ever so slightly, offering her the subtlest of smiles. "If you would like to overcome your fear, now is a good time. I will walk behind you. If you are too afraid, stop and turn around. I'll lead you back down," he said.

Peyton imagined how beautiful the view would be and that it was likely her only chance to see it, so she agreed.

The group slowly made their way up the staircase, along with other tourists. Liev kept his promise, following Peyton and reminding her they could head back if needed. In the beginning she was anxious, her palms sweaty and mind racing, but she took deep breaths at the suggestion of Harper and Ariana. Contrary to her fear, the higher they got, the less nervous she felt. By the time they reached the top, she was exhilarated. As she took the last step up, the group began clapping. Peyton blushed. She turned to Liev and said, "Thank you." He smiled and said, "You're quite welcome. Today is always better than someday."

They all walked to the spot with the clearest view.

"We should take a group picture," Harper suggested. She handed her phone to Dietrich. "Your arms are longer than mine."

They smooshed together for a group selfie.

"I'll send it to all of you," Harper said.

"It's really spectacular, isn't it?" Ronnie said.

Everyone agreed.

"And look," Harper said. "There are so many rainbows."

Peyton grinned like a Cheshire cat. "Rainbows have seven colors."

Chapter 9

* * *

As Aldar pulled up to Crystal Manor, Milton turned back and said, "Sleepyheads, we're back." He then looked at Aldar and said, "They say us old guys nap a lot, but we're the only ones who stayed awake." They both chuckled.

Harper slowly sat up to realize she had fallen asleep on Dietrich's shoulder. "Oh, I'm sorry," she said softly.

"Quite all right. I dozed off too."

Peyton opened her eyes, smiling at the sight of the sparkling estate. She turned to Ronnie, "I'm surprised I fell asleep."

"You must have been relaxed. Personally, I feel like I could sleep for ages. My body is totally zapped," Ronnie said.

"It may take you a while to build your energy up," Peyton said.

"Yes, you are depleted," Liev added before yawning.

Everyone gathered their belongings and disembarked, stretching their arms and necks.

Peyton said, "Well, I'm going to bring my things to my room and record some notes from today. See you all at dinner."

"I'm heading to my room too," Liev said, followed by Ronnie, Milton, and Ariana.

"I think I'll walk around for a bit, wake myself up," Harper said.

"Would you like company?" Dietrich asked.

"Sure."

Dietrich and Harper retreated to the back of the property while everyone else went inside.

✳   ✳   ✳

It's strange we are so comfortable together, Dietrich thought as he and Harper walked along the seaside edge of the estate.

"Is this where you've been running in the mornings?" he asked.

"Yes, just around the bend, there's a path through the trees," she said, pointing ahead.

"Perhaps I'll join you tomorrow. I could use some exercise."

"Lovely. I'll meet you at that bench."

"May I ask you something?" he said.

"Sure."

"I've been thinking about what you said about Helmut, my brother. How our pursuits were not as disparate as I thought."

"Yes, I remember," Harper said.

"You have a very different way of looking at things than I do. I know we didn't initially understand each other, but now I feel compelled to consider what you say carefully, and I wanted to tell you I value your point of view. It challenges me. It makes me, uh . . ." He glanced down, searching for the words.

"Question things, perhaps?"

"Yes. Precisely," he replied.

"I'm glad. You do the same for me. Suspect it's why we're here, really," she said.

"Hmm. Yes, I suppose so, one way or another," he said.

Harper smiled. "Oh gee, I just realized I should run inside to practice a bit."

"Practice what?" Dietrich asked.

"I was asked to do a short performance tonight, after dinner. Slipped my mind. I'm going to skip dinner, I never eat right before a show."

"You're going to dance?"

"Yeah, and I better go warm up," she said, trotting off with a wave.

"Good luck!" he hollered after her. *I know you'll be marvelous.*

* * *

Peyton entered her room and unpacked her bag, smiling as she took out her scarf and hand sanitizer. *It was worth bringing all of this to be able to help out Harper and Ronnie.* She tossed her notebook on the bed, snatched her laptop, and plopped down. *I better transcribe as many of my notes as possible while they're fresh in my mind. As usual, it didn't seem productive, but you never know.*

She proceeded to type up her notes, adding as many details as she could remember, and separating observations from impressions to the best of her ability. She stared at the typed notes desperately hoping for a lightning bolt and fearful that they were no closer to completing their task. In the end, she was left with two questions: *Were Ronnie and Ariana on to something when they discussed the continents? How could Liev be so sympathetic to me and Ronnie and so infuriating to work with?*

* * *

On her way to dinner, Peyton bumped into Diego.

"Hello, Peyton. How was your excursion?" he asked.

"The scenery was exquisite. I've always wanted to visit Iceland, and it doesn't disappoint. We saw something interesting too. You know the paintings on display here, with the bodies in the mountains?"

"Yes," he replied.

"At the tectonic plates we saw faces in the rocks. The faces seemed to be in nearly all of them. Do I sound crazy?" she asked.

Diego smiled, flexing his dimples. "I would never think such a thing. When we are open, there is always the chance to see something new, something wondrous we may have missed before."

That's a nice thing to say, she thought.

"May I ask you something?" he asked.

"Yes," she said.

"You are becoming more comfortable here, yes?"

She nodded. "I just . . . I just don't know if we're making progress. What will happen if we fail? We were brought here to answer one question. What if we can't answer it?"

"I wouldn't worry about that. Trust the process. You can't control the outcome. But I do not think failure is possible."

"Thanks. That makes me feel a little better."

"Please, join your friends for dinner. I didn't mean to detain you."

"Thank you, Diego. Have a good night."

As he was walking away Peyton said, "One more thing, Diego, if you have a minute."

"Of course."

"For some reason my group was talking about the number seven today. It just occurred to me that we work for five days and then leave on the morning of the sixth day. I'm curious, why six days? Why isn't the institute a full week?"

"Because we need one day to prepare for the others."

"The others?"

"The next group."

"Ah, I see," Peyton said. "Thank you."

"My pleasure. Enjoy dinner."

They parted ways. As Peyton approached the dining room she began to wonder what the next group would be tasked with. *Is it possible they will be answering the same question?*

*   *   *

Peyton walked into the bustling dining hall. Clusters of people were standing around the buffet engrossed in conversations about the sights they'd seen, while others were gabbing away at their tables. Everyone seemed more jubilant than evenings before, and the sound of laughter ping-ponged across the room. Peyton looked around until she saw Ronnie, Milton, and Dietrich sitting together with a couple of people from other groups. She waved, and Ronnie motioned that she was saving her a seat. Peyton went to the buffet first, selecting Icelandic stew and a green salad. She headed toward her friends, exchanging smiles with several participants along the way. Liev crossed her path and she dipped her head, to acknowledge him. He stopped in her path.

"Peyton, today was fun. It's a fascinating country," he said.

"Yeah. We're so lucky to be here. I felt like pinching myself all day."

Liev smiled. "And you conquered your fear. Now you must feel you can do anything."

"Oh, I don't know about that. Maybe. Thank you for helping me."

"Don't mention it. Remember, today is always better than someday," he said before walking away.

Peyton joined her friends. "Where's Harper?" she asked.

"Dietrich said she's doing a performance after dinner. She must be rehearsing," Ronnie said.

Dietrich nodded. "Harper doesn't like to eat before a performance. I'm going to fix her a small plate of food for later. Juliette is bringing me something to cover the plate."

"That's extremely thoughtful of you," Peyton said.

"You two sure have gotten real close," Ronnie said.

Dietrich fidgeted with his glasses.

Ronnie turned to Peyton. "You and me are like peas in a pod and they're like peas and carrots."

Dietrich twitched his nose. "Ah, well . . ."

"It will be a treat to see her dance," Peyton said.

Everyone smiled and refocused on dinner.

"This smells good," Peyton said before taking a bite of stew.

"It's great," Milton said, as he ran a piece of bread across his plate to sop up the hearty sauce.

"I decided to try something I wouldn't normally get to have," Peyton said.

Ronnie smiled. "Seems like your day for trying new things. I was really impressed you made it up to the top of the waterfall."

Peyton blushed. "Funny, Liev and I were just talking about that. I can't quite figure him out."

"He was real sweet to me today when I didn't feel well, and to you too, but boy oh boy he's stubborn," Ronnie said.

"Yeah, but I'm beginning to wonder . . ."

"What?" Ronnie asked.

"If we can't find some common ground."

"I don't know if we have any common ground," Ronnie said.

"Maybe we can find a way to create one," Peyton said.

✳   ✳   ✳

Peyton and Ronnie were among the first to arrive in the music hall for the evening presentations. Dietrich was already sitting in the front row, holding a plate covered in tinfoil. They sat next to him, ready to cheer Harper on. People filed in, carrying glasses of wine and beer from dinner. As the empty seats filled, the cheerful noise from conversations grew into a cacophony of sound.

Ronnie leaned over to Peyton. "Everyone sure is upbeat tonight. This is the most abundant positive energy since we got here."

"From what I overheard in the dining room, everyone had an amazing time today. How could you not? It's such a spectacular place."

"Seems people have loosened up too, now that we're in the swing of things and all know each other better. By the looks of it tonight, I think folks are making friends for life, like us," Ronnie said.

Peyton smiled and turned to the front of the room where Ms. Goodright surreptitiously took to the podium. "Good evening."

Peyton looked around as everyone continued talking and laughing. She inadvertently made eye contact with Liev, a few rows behind on the other side of the room. He winked at her. *Hmm, he's perplexing,* she thought.

Ms. Goodright tapped the microphone, getting everyone's attention. "Good evening, I know we're all getting settled in but we'd like to start the program," she said, ushering in quiet. "Today you were all exposed to some of the natural wonders of this country. Tonight's presentations celebrate our landscape. You will see two special presentations that offer different ways of understanding the majesty you saw today. First we will be treated to a geological lecture and slide presentation. We will conclude with a dance performance inspired by Icelandic nature. After the presentations I do hope you will take pleasure in the facilities for some recreational time. Please, make your colleagues feel welcome."

Dietrich slid the plate under his seat as everyone began clapping. Ms. Goodright left the podium, taking a seat in the back of the room. A local professor of geology offered a fascinating lecture on Iceland's tumultuous landscape, with slides depicting icebergs, volcanoes, aerial views of fault lines, thermal baths, and other feats of nature. He concluded, "You can see why Iceland is known as the land of fire and ice. And, yes, music lovers, Björk was quite astute, these landscapes are indeed emotional. I think that will be highlighted in the performance."

Peyton's heart raced with excitement. *The land of fire and ice. That's what it said in the invitation letter we received. Am I beginning to understand?*

Ms. Goodright turned off all of the lights. After a moment, a soft light lit the stage. Harper, dressed in a black leotard and translucent skirt, was curled up in a ball at the center of the stage. The sound of a lone piano key broke the silence. As Harper began to slowly unfurl her limbs, Peyton turned to Dietrich, to notice the corners of his mouth turned almost imperceptibly upward. *He's smitten. When we first met I never would have put them together.* She tapped Ronnie, who glanced over, and they both smiled. Everyone was mesmerized during the performance. Harper was one with the music, gracefully moving like mist in the air, eventually building into thunderous waterfalls. She soared across the stage in volcanic eruptions as the music swelled and finally returned to a ball center stage as the sparse music softened. One lone piano key signaled the end of the performance. Everyone leapt to their feet, cheering. Peyton turned around to see the audience. Liev was standing and clapping.

The lights came on and people started stirring about. Peyton and Ronnie approached Harper.

"Wow! That was amazing!" Ronnie exclaimed.

"It was so beautiful. I loved it. You really captured how I felt today," Peyton said.

"Glad to hear it. I had fun. Love using nature as inspiration," Harper replied.

"Me too," Ronnie said.

"The lecture was also fascinating," Peyton said.

"Yeah. Learned a lot," Harper said.

"But the feelings, you brought those to life, Harper. That's what we artists strive to do," Ronnie said.

Harper smiled.

"I think everyone is going to hang out. Dietrich brought you some food," Peyton said.

"That's lovely," Harper said, motioning for him to come over.

"I didn't want to interrupt," Dietrich said.

"You're not," Harper replied.

"Your dance was beautiful. I thoroughly enjoyed it," he said.

Harper smiled. "Everyone seems to be going down to the pub. Should we join 'em?"

"Listen, guys, I hate to be a party pooper again but I'm really wiped. My body's taken a beating," Ronnie said.

"Oh, you poor thing," Harper said.

"It's been such a great day. Can you come for a little while?" Peyton asked.

"Sure," Ronnie replied.

I wonder if I should get that bottle of wine for Liev? Something shifted today. I should make an effort. But if Ronnie is only staying for a little while, I don't want to miss all being together. The wine can keep I guess, Peyton thought.

They made their way down to the pub along with the others. Peyton noticed the room was toasty warm.

"Look, Milton's at that back table, waving us over," Ronnie said.

Harper sat next to Milton. "Thanks for saving seats."

Milton nodded. "Nice job," he said before taking a sip of beer.

Harper rubbed Milton's arm and tilted her chin by way of saying thank you.

Dietrich slid the plate in front of Harper. She peeled back the foil wrap to find an array of meticulously arranged cheeses, fruit, and crackers. "I remember how much you liked the cheese the other day. And I know you eat light after a performance. I hope this is all right."

"It's perfect. Thank you."

"I'm getting a beer. What would you like to drink?" he asked.

"Water and a white wine, please," she said.

He turned to the others. "What can I get you, Ronnie and Peyton?"

"Water for me, thanks," Ronnie said.

"Me too, but I'll come help," Peyton said.

Dietrich grabbed a few drinks and headed back to the table. Peyton stood at the bar taking stock of the room. Literature professors laughed hysterically at something a composer said, a poet wrangled a scientist to go play in the game room, and her friends clinked their glasses. It all warmed her from the inside. She grabbed a bag of potato chips, about to rejoin her friends, when Liev emerged from the game room, walking straight to the bar.

"Were you playing a game?" she asked.

"Not tonight, but some others are playing table tennis if you want to join them," he replied, snagging a bottle of water from the cooler.

"What did you think of the presentations tonight?" she asked.

"Terrific," he said.

"Harper is a wonderful dancer," she prodded.

"She is quite talented."

"The contrast between the slide presentation and dance was interesting. I felt Harper really captured the feeling of the landscapes," Peyton said.

"Indeed. Naturally it's not informative in the way a lecture is, but I appreciate what she does. It has its place. Good night," he said.

"You're going to bed so early?" Peyton asked.

"I must rest. See you tomorrow."

Peyton smiled, surveying the room again, trying to soak up the moment. *Well, he liked the dance. Maybe we're getting somewhere after all,* she thought as she popped a chip into her mouth.

Chapter 10

*   *   *

Peyton's alarm went off at the crack of dawn. Her anxiety abated and feeling full of hope, she wanted ample time to review all of her notes. *We said we'd tackle the question directly today. How exactly can we do that? What is something we had in common?* She scrolled through her notes. *Hmm, we were all on the same page when talking about environmental science at the waterfall yesterday. What exactly did we say?* Peyton began highlighting bits that leapt out at her:

dinosaur thinking
a new way to think

That's it. We're each sort of stuck in dinosaur thinking. We need to develop a new way to think. But how do we do that? Draw from what you know, Peyton. You're here for a reason. Think. Okay, what would I do in my own work? What would I do if I had a sociological research problem? That's it! I've got an idea.

*   *   *

Dietrich turned the corner to see Harper stretching her legs on a bench. "Hope I didn't keep you waiting," he called.

"Not at all. It's gorgeous isn't it? Cold, but exhilarating," she replied.

"Yes," he said. "I hope I don't slow you down, I'm not fast."

"That's all right. Glad for the company," she said.

"I was thinking about how things might go today, in the sessions later," he said.

"Yeah, I think we all are."

"I'm not sure that there is an answer to the question, or a way for our group to figure it out. We only have a couple days left," Dietrich said.

"Yesterday when we were all at the top of Gullfoss I had the feeling it would all work out. Even though I don't know how."

"Yes. Something changed yesterday. Please don't tell Peyton I said this, but I think her fear of heights was helpful."

Harper scrunched her face.

"It forced us to accomplish something together. Does that make sense?"

"Yeah. You're right."

Dietrich smiled.

Harper bent over to tighten her shoelace. "Okay, shall we have a go? Last one back to the bench is a rotten egg."

*　　　*　　　*

Peyton's stomach growled as she entered the grand hall. She had her laptop in a tote bag but headed straight to the buffet to get oatmeal and fruit before searching for her friends. Ronnie, Harper, Dietrich, and Milton were sitting together. Peyton practically skipped over to join them.

"You sure are perky this morning," Ronnie said.

"Oh, well, I just had a great time yesterday and I'm looking forward to whatever happens next."

"Same here," Harper said.

"And here," Dietrich said.

"Can't wait for the Blue Lagoon tomorrow. It's supposed to be healing," Harper said.

Peyton smiled and took a bite of her banana.

"Hey, guys, I feel terrible but I don't think I can go with you tomorrow," Ronnie said.

"But you've been looking forward to seeing the Blue Lagoon," Peyton said, as her heart dropped.

"It kills me but after how miserable I was yesterday, I don't want to risk being sick on the ride there."

Harper dropped her apple. "Oh no! Won't be the same without you."

"I wish there was something we could do to help," Peyton said.

"Thanks, guys," Ronnie said.

"Ronnie, don't make a decision yet," Milton said.

Ronnie opened her mouth to respond but Milton continued, "I think I know what's been making you sick. Give me a few minutes. I'm going into the kitchen. Don't eat anything."

Ronnie shrugged and slumped over, already defeated.

"Cheer up, Ronnie," Peyton whispered.

Milton got up and walked away, leaving everyone bewildered. He returned a few minutes later, sat down, and took a sip of his orange juice. "Why do people always ask which came first, the chicken or the egg?" he asked.

"What?" Peyton asked.

Ronnie perked up to listen.

"I love eggs. They're the perfect food. And I've raised chickens most of my life and I'll never understand why people always ask that," he said.

Confused, Peyton and Ronnie glanced at each other.

"One of life's mysteries, huh, Milton?" Harper said.

Milton ignored her and continued. "Chickens are pretty easy to keep. The first chickens I got arrived in a box when they were just two days old. Think about that. The hatchery in Pennsylvania puts little chicks in a box the day they hatch. The box travels by mail to my farm with the chicks peeping and getting jostled about. When I get them I take them out of the box one at a time and dip their beaks in the water holder so they know where to get a drink. Then I let them loose. They usually take a short run, stop for a bit, then run again. I have a heat lamp hanging over one part of their pen, and there's a feeder. The heat lamp is to make a place that's warm enough to make them comfortable. If their mother was around the chicks would run under her wings whenever they felt cold."

Milton stared at a sea of perplexed faces. He took another sip of juice and continued. "You may be surprised and disappointed when I tell you what makes the tastiest eggs."

Ronnie interjected before he could continue. "Milton, this is real interesting and I can see you're passionate about chickens but . . ."

Milton interrupted. "Let me tell you what makes the best eggs, most people don't know."

"Sure thing, Milton," Ronnie said.

Peyton smiled awkwardly.

"Well there are three things to consider: what goes into the chicken that she turns into eggs, what happens to the egg after it is laid, and the breed of chicken. Chickens are omnivores. They'll eat just about anything. Chickens in a barnyard are frequently seen scratching around a cow flop. They're not eating manure, though most likely some is ingested, they're actually eating maggots. Flies lay eggs in the manure, eggs hatch out maggots who eat the manure, and when chickens are around they eat the maggots, thereby cutting down the fly population. Pretty significantly, I might add. Scratching around the manure also spreads out those nutrients, improving soil fertility, which grows good grass, the best feed for cows. Cycle of life."

"Uh, wow. That's really something, Milton," Ronnie said.

"It's kind of gross," Peyton lamented.

"When you start gardening you learn some things you didn't want to think about," Harper said.

Milton nodded. "Most people have no idea where their food comes from."

"Nature is a perfect system though, eh?" Harper replied.

"It is. And I haven't even gotten to egg quality and what makes for the most delicious eggs," Milton said.

Peyton looked around. It seemed she wasn't alone and that none of them understood what precipitated this ramble, although they all smiled politely. Milton had never been so animated.

"I feed my chickens organic chicken feed. I think it makes a difference in the health of the chickens. But the truth is, I don't know if it makes a difference in the flavor of the eggs. You can tell a lot from the color of the yolk. It should be a dark, rich color, not the pale yellow you see in store-bought eggs."

"Like a sunset, not a sunrise," Ronnie said.

"Yup," Milton replied.

"You always think like an artist," Peyton said.

Ronnie smiled.

Milton continued, "Anyway, you'll notice when an egg comes from a chicken that has been able to forage on grassland, the yolk will be a deep orange bordering on red. In Maine, I see the color of the yolks get less intense when winter forces them inside. Chickens don't lay much in the winter; production slows down when the days start getting shorter and picks up again in the spring. I've learned to stock up on eggs when production slows down, especially when my chickens are getting older and laying less. I hear people say freshness is important but I would rather eat a three-month-old egg from my own chickens than a store-bought egg."

Everyone nodded.

"Even though all of these things probably have an influence, my wife and I agree that the breed of chicken makes the biggest difference in how eggs taste. Leghorns are popular because they produce a lot of eggs. But we like the Rhode Island Reds. They produce the tastiest eggs."

"Milton, this is all real interesting. Thanks for teaching us so much. I'm not sure it helps my predicament, but I love learning new things," Ronnie said.

Milton smiled. "The eggs are making you sick, Ronnie."

"What? Why do you think that? You think they're bad?" she asked.

"But I've been eating eggs and I'm fine," Harper said.

"The eggs aren't bad, they're contaminated with gluten. I've observed everything you've eaten, and I developed a hunch. The first time you got sick was after dinner the first night. You thought it was the rice crackers. It wasn't the crackers. What actually made you sick was the chopped liver pâté, which contained pieces of hard-boiled eggs. The next morning you had a hard-boiled egg and a banana because you were afraid to eat anything else. You got sick again. You thought it was still from the night before, but it wasn't. Then for lunch you had soft-boiled eggs and got sick again. Yesterday the sandwich you ate had sliced hard-boiled eggs in it. You didn't even consider eggs because they're naturally gluten free, but it's the eggs. I'm certain as I can be."

"But how?" Ronnie asked.

"Well, that's why I went into the kitchen. To test my theory. Every night they boil noodles for the buffet. The next morning, they use the same pot to boil the eggs, without washing it. For someone as sensitive as you, Ronnie, that'd do it. They have a new assistant in the kitchen who didn't realize the misstep."

Jaws dropped open.

Milton gulped down the rest of his juice.

"Milton, you're a genius!" Ronnie proclaimed.

Milton shrugged.

"Fascinating. You're quite the detective. So does cracking the shell create the contamination problem, or is it because the shells are porous?" Harper asked.

"Well, let me tell you all about eggshells. For starters, people have all of these ideas about the color of the shell."

Chapter 11

*   *   *

After finishing breakfast, Peyton and her friends stopped at Liev and Ariana's table. They all walked to the library together. Peyton purposely sat in the chair nearest to the easel. Ronnie, Milton, Ariana, and Liev sat in the remaining chairs. Harper plopped onto the loveseat, crossing her legs, and Dietrich sat beside her. Peyton pulled her laptop out of her bag, flipped it on, and placed it on the table.

"So, yesterday was wonderful. What is our plan for today?" Ariana asked.

I should tell them my idea, Peyton thought, looking at Ronnie for courage.

"Since we free-flowed it yesterday, maybe we should tackle things more directly today," Ronnie suggested.

Now's my chance. "I have an idea," Peyton said.

"The floor is yours," Ariana said, smiling warmly.

"Well, it occurred to me that we've all been viewing the question from different lenses because of the kind of work we each do, which Ariana pointed out early on. But we've been relying on our own experiences and impressions. I started to think about how in my field I would approach a question or problem. I would bring in examples from other experts. I wouldn't just rely on my own limited knowledge."

"Yes, I would do this too, if only to make my point," Liev said.

"Me as well," Dietrich said.

Peyton smiled. "We are fortunate to be in the library today. Let's take advantage."

"What do you propose?" Liev asked.

"Let's designate the morning segment to individually researching each of our fields. Then after the break we can share the information we've collected," Peyton said.

"What exactly would we be searching for?" Harper inquired.

"Here, let me use the pad to show you," Peyton said, standing as she picked up a black magic marker. In the center of a fresh sheet of paper she wrote:

How do you approach a question or problem?

"So, we would each research common ways of answering questions or solving problems in our field. We'll take as many notes as possible. I brought my computer to transcribe everything when we each share what we've learned."

"How will we use the information we gather?" Dietrich asked.

"I'm not exactly sure, but I'm hoping we might see some synergies across our fields. We each have a specific way we see things. If we put them together in some kind of organized way, maybe we can build one approach to problem solving."

"I think that's a good plan," Ariana said.

"I'm just a little confused about how I would do this," Harper said. "I see how scholars can do this, but as a dancer, I've never worked that way. Where would I begin?"

"Are there different approaches to choreography?" Ronnie asked. "If you want to create a dance about something, are there different ways of building the dance? I bet you could find a bunch of stuff."

"Yeah, I see what you mean," Harper said.

Dietrich cleared his throat. "Perhaps you could look at philosophies of what can be learned through dance and movement. There's quite a lot written on embodiment perspectives."

"That might work, too," Harper said.

Dietrich turned to face Harper. "If you like, it would be my pleasure to help you. I'm a good researcher, and I've read a bit about embodiment."

Harper smiled. "Thanks."

"Is anyone else concerned about how this will work?" Ariana asked.

Everyone glanced at Milton.

He snorted. "I'm good. I've been reading about farming and agriculture longer than some of you have been alive."

"Well then, should we give it a try?" Ariana asked.

"Let's begin," Liev said.

For the next hour and a half everyone dispersed into the library stacks and online databases. After a short break for refreshments, they returned to their seats to share what they had learned. One by one, they each took a turn writing down main points from their research on a fresh sheet of paper. At Peyton's suggestion, they each summarized what they had learned in a sentence at the bottom of the sheet.

"Would somebody be willing to put it all together on one sheet, while I transcribe everything onto my laptop?" Peyton asked.

"I'll do it," Ariana said.

Ariana turned to a fresh page. In the center she wrote and circled:

How do you approach a question or problem?

She drew seven lines out of the circle. At the end of each line she wrote each participant's summary statement.

"Maybe you should put a square around each one," Ronnie suggested.

"Good idea," Ariana said as she proceeded to box in each statement.

"Let's start noting connections," Peyton suggested.

"We should label differences as well," Liev said.

"If you use different colors it would be easier for us visual folks to follow," Ronnie said.

"How about I put red arrows between connections and blue dotted lines between differences?" Ariana suggested.

Everyone agreed.

As people started calling out observations, Ariana filled in the map. They continued this process after lunch, making several new versions of the map, each of which Peyton recorded. At one point Liev and Dietrich began verbal sparring over the strength of certain connections. Liev was insistent connections derive from linear thinking and discernable facts. Dietrich advocated a more open, dialectical, and philosophical approach. They went back and forth, their voices growing in strength in direct proportion to their stubbornness. Neither would back down. When they began to take it further and question the legitimacy of some points, Ariana suggested, "This process may work more effectively if we accept differing viewpoints as valid and work outward from that assumption." With a few grumbles, the group got back on track, and before long it was tea time.

✳   ✳   ✳

They made their way to the lounge for tea, joining other participants engaged in relaxed chatter. Peyton found herself standing next to Liev at the refreshment stand. He was wrapping a couple of finger sandwiches in a napkin. She inadvertently stared at him.

"I have to run to my room before the final segment," he said.

"Ah," Peyton replied.

"You seemed quite timid when we first arrived here and began our work," he said.

"Uh, well, I guess I'm shy," she replied.

"Today you steered the group. See, I told you that once you conquered your fear you would feel like you could do anything."

"Oh, well, um . . . "

Liev smiled.

"I guess I'm starting to find my way," Peyton said.

"Indeed. I'll see you back in the library," he said, before dashing off.

I wish I didn't always sound so incoherent around him. Even when he's trying to compliment me he has this way of wording it that makes me wonder if he thinks I'm stupid. Maybe it's me. I read too much into things.

Peyton poured a cup of tea and joined Ronnie and Ariana, who were sitting together in a quiet corner of the room.

"Ronnie and I were just saying that today has been productive. Your idea was excellent," Ariana said.

"I'm glad it finally feels like we're getting somewhere. And thank you for always helping to move things forward. You're so skilled at that," Peyton replied.

"Yeah, you sure are good at handling Liev," Ronnie said.

Ariana smiled. "Survival strategy, I suppose."

"I honestly can't figure him out," Peyton said. "When I first got here I thought he was, uh, well . . . "

"An arrogant, condescending know-it-all?" Ariana asked with a chuckle.

"Exactly," Ronnie said.

Peyton nodded. "It's bewildering. I have to admit that when I heard him lecture the other night, I was captivated. Is he a genius in your field?"

"He is many things. In his work, he's bold and innovative. I admire that. He's also arrogant. Usually his colleagues only get to see those sides of him, but this is an unusual circumstance, after all, so you are seeing some of his softer sides too," Ariana replied.

"When I first met him I thought that he doesn't seem to listen to others, and I wondered if you find him kind of sexist," Peyton said.

Ariana laughed. "That's the norm in my profession. They are often oblivious to it. Suits them to be so."

"That must be difficult, huh?" Peyton said.

"I'm a woman of color from south of the equator in a field dominated by white, Western men. That is my reality."

Peyton inhaled deeply, contemplating Ariana's words.

"It must be infuriating!" Ronnie exclaimed.

"It is. Liev has been an important mentor in some ways so it's complicated. I'm forced to negotiate multiple realities."

Peyton sighed.

"He's gotten both better and worse since his illness," Ariana said.

"Illness?" Peyton asked.

"He was very sick a few years ago. He beat it, but now it's back. That's why he just left. He ran to his room to take his medication. He was always impatient, and time is not on his side. I think that's why he pushes so hard. And he's angry that it took a long time, too long, for people to accept his work. There's nothing worse to him than wasted time. He's afraid of what will happen to his work when he's gone. He's devoted everything to his scientific legacy."

Peyton shook her head.

"Well, that sure explains some things," Ronnie said.

"Like what?" Ariana asked.

"How frustrated he got with Harper at lunch yesterday when our conversation veered off some, but how sweet he was to me when I didn't feel well."

"And to me when I was hesitating at the waterfall," Peyton added.

"Yes, I can see that," Ariana said.

"What he said to me at the waterfall and then again last night, that someday is dangerous and today is always better than someday," Peyton said.

"Today is everything to him. What he does each today gives his body of work another tomorrow, even though he won't be here to see it," Ariana said.

"Hmm. It's interesting," Peyton muttered.

"What?" Ronnie asked.

"That he chose to come here, to give his time to this seminar. He must have felt it was important. I feel it too. Whatever we're doing here matters. It really matters."

Soon a chime indicated it was time for the final segment. The group returned to the library and picked up where they left off, fleshing out synergies, drawing new maps, and trying to create a unified framework out of it all. Although her plan was working even better than she had imagined, Peyton was distracted. *We're still missing something. Just like I was with Liev and Ariana too. There's something I'm not seeing.*

Chapter 12

✳   ✳   ✳

Peyton arrived early to dinner. The staff was still placing the last items on the buffet. She selected the table nearest the food, poured a glass of water, and waited, eager to talk to Ronnie. People started meandering in. Milton was the first of her friends to arrive, followed by Harper, Dietrich, and Ronnie.

"Over here," Peyton called.

"You beat me here!" Ronnie said.

"I really wanted to talk to you."

"Everything okay?" Ronnie asked.

"Yeah, I just want to talk about today."

"Should we get some grub first?" Ronnie asked.

Peyton nodded, and they headed to the buffet. Ronnie piled her plate high with roast turkey, mashed potatoes, and vegetables. When Peyton took a scoop of rice, Ronnie held out her plate and said, "Hit me with one of those, will ya?"

Peyton smiled. "It's good to see you have an appetite."

"I'm ravenous. Now that I'm not worried about getting sick I'm making up for lost time."

They returned to their table to find a few more people had joined them. Soon they were swept away in a table-wide conversation that took them from philosophy to film. Before they knew it, Milton was having his second slice of pie.

Ronnie tapped Peyton's arm. "Hey, you wanted to talk about something."

Peyton opened her mouth but Ronnie continued, "Is it about Liev? Hard to believe such a powerhouse is also frail."

Peyton nodded.

"And Ariana, how about what she said?" Ronnie continued.

"Yeah, I know," Peyton said.

"That was eye-opening," Ronnie said. "Women in the arts are always fighting uphill. I feel badly for saying this, but I didn't think about how much more complicated it was for her as a woman of color, in the sciences no less. I was complicit too. When we first met, I saw her as Liev's sidekick."

Peyton nodded. "Me too. I should know better."

"I'm really starting to like her. I mistakenly lumped her in with Liev, personality wise, but she's definitely her own person, nothing like him even if they have some of the same views," Ronnie said.

"Uh huh. I did the same thing. I like her too. She's smart. But actually that's not what I need to talk to you about. It's about the group and our final report."

"Today was great. It finally felt like we were getting somewhere," Ronnie said.

Peyton inhaled.

"You don't think so?" Ronnie asked.

"No, today was good, it's just . . ."

Peyton was interrupted as suddenly Ms. Goodright addressed the room from in front of the buffet.

"Good evening, everyone," she said.

"We'll talk after," Peyton whispered.

"I hope you all had a productive day. I'm sure you're looking forward to your excursions tomorrow. The vans will depart immediately after breakfast. For those groups traveling to the Blue Lagoon, please bring your swimwear and any personal items you may need.

You will be given towels, robes, and sandals at the Lagoon. All groups will return in advance of afternoon tea, allowing you time to stop in your rooms. After tea all groups will participate in the last segment of the seminar. Your brief final reports are due the following morning. Scribes may submit them via email. Are there any questions?"

People looked around, mumbling, but no one asked anything, so Ms. Goodright continued.

"We know how hard you've been working. Tonight we have something special planned. A local band will be playing in the Music Hall. As you will see, we've set up a dance floor. Please, take your drinks and go enjoy yourselves. As always, the pub is also available to you."

With those words Ms. Goodright exited the room.

Milton stood up. "Should we head over?"

"Yeah, let's go have some fun," Harper added.

Ronnie looked at Peyton and mouthed, "Want to talk?"

Peyton shook her head. "It's all right. It can wait until the morning."

"I'll meet you early at breakfast, okay?" Ronnie said.

Peyton smiled. "Thanks."

"So I guess we should go get our groove on," Ronnie said with a laugh.

Peyton winced.

"Come on, it'll be a hoot," Ronnie said, standing up.

Peyton shrugged, gulped the rest of her water, and stood up. "I guess it'll be fun to see everyone dance."

"That's the spirit!" Ronnie said.

Peyton laughed. "You're the best."

*　　　*　　　*

Peyton and Ronnie joined the others to find the band was in full swing. A few people were already on the dance floor, while others milled around the perimeter of the room. There were picnic tables against one wall with water, beer, bottles of wine, and bowls of pretzels and nuts. People were drinking, laughing, and enjoying the music.

I should get that bottle of wine for Liev, Peyton thought.

"Hey, guys," Harper hollered from one of the tables.

"Let's go over and watch the band," Ronnie said.

Peyton nodded. *I guess the wine can wait.*

They joined Harper, Dietrich, and Milton, who were listening to the music.

"They're good, aren't they?" Harper said, swaying from side to side.

Everyone agreed. Dietrich grabbed a fistful of nuts and a beer.

"Don't get too comfortable. We're going to dance," Harper said.

Dietrich gulped. "Uh, oh, I don't really know how to dance."

"Good thing I'm a dance teacher," Harper replied.

Dietrich blushed.

"After your beer," Harper said.

Peyton found the exchange sweet. *I'd be so embarrassed if someone made me dance. But then I'd regret it all night if I didn't. I bet he has fun. They seem good for each other. Never would have thought that on the first day.* Her thoughts faded as she got lost in the music. Soon nearly everyone was on the dance floor, even Liev. He and a literature professor were doing something that resembled square dancing, though totally unburdened by rhythm.

"That's it," Harper said turning to Dietrich. "You'll nurse that all night if I let ya. If Liev can dance, so can you."

Dietrich's cheeks reddened, but he put his beer down and took Harper's hand.

Peyton loved watching everyone so much that she didn't realize she was alone at the table. Ronnie and Milton motioned to her from the dance floor, but she shook her head. Ariana walked over to her, sat on the bench, and reached for the pitcher. She poured a glass of water and quickly drank the whole thing.

"Hot out there," she said.

"Looks fun," Peyton said.

"Fun and funny. Look at these people flailing about. Hard to believe they are some of the most brilliant people in the world. It's disarming and wonderful."

Peyton smiled. "Yeah, they're not quite as intimidating now."

"I hope it doesn't end up on YouTube! Although I could use clips of it in my standup act," Ariana said.

Peyton laughed.

"Come on. Let's join them. Just for a few minutes," Ariana said.

Peyton looked at the dance floor—there was joy and freedom. She wanted to be a part of it. She took a deep breath and said, "Okay."

They stood up and shimmied their way to Ronnie and Milton. Harper pulled Dietrich over and a couple minutes later Liev joined them. "Seems our group is together," he shouted over the music.

With smiles across their faces, and no regard for the beat, they danced.

Chapter 13

*　　*　　*

Peyton walked into the dining hall twenty minutes before the start of breakfast, a tote bag on her shoulder and worry on her mind. She was elated to see Ronnie waiting for her.

"Thanks for coming to meet me," Peyton said as she sat down, dropping her bag on the floor.

"Of course! That's what pals are for. I'm on my second latte."

Peyton smiled.

"What's up?" Ronnie asked.

"Today is the last day and I'm afraid we're not going to answer the question."

"Yesterday was our best day yet," Ronnie said.

"I know. But even though we were much more productive and didn't step on each other's toes, I'm not sure we're really getting at the question. I still don't think we've figured out exactly what we're being asked. Something is missing and we're running out of time."

"We still have another meeting at the end of the day," Ronnie said.

"I don't think that's enough," Peyton said, furrowing her brow.

"I hear ya. I have concerns too. What do you want to do?" Ronnie asked.

"The Blue Lagoon. I know everyone is looking forward to it, and I am too. I mean, I've always wanted to go there, but we have to convince them to work while we're there. At least part of the time."

Ronnie nodded. "Okay, I'm with ya."

"I'm scared they might resist. I don't think everyone understands the pressure I feel being responsible for the report."

"Don't worry. I've got your back and we won't take no for an answer."

"Thanks, Ronnie."

"You bet ya. People are starting to come in. Should we grab some fuel?"

"Sure," Peyton said.

*　　*　　*

Although tired from the night before, everyone eagerly hopped into the van, excited for the day.

"There won't be much to see for most of the ride I'm afraid, we'll be on the highway. There are nootka lupine lining the road though," Aldar said.

Peyton watched as they drove away from the estate and then turned to Ronnie, who smiled at her. Peyton cocked her head and they both leaned back, gazing out their windows.

"I can't believe this is our last day," Harper said softly to Dietrich.

"Yes, it's, uh, difficult to think about going home," Dietrich said.

Harper frowned. "Guess I'm lucky I'm not heading back yet. Though I'm not sure how to leave you all."

The faintest smile ran across Dietrich's face. "Have you decided where you're going tomorrow? You mentioned you might visit friends in Europe or the United States."

"I rented a car. Gonna do some sightseeing here. Can't bear to leave yet. Not sure after that."

Dietrich glanced down. "What is it?" she asked.

"Can we talk privately back at the estate?"

"Sure. Come to my room after the last segment, before dinner." Dietrich smiled.

Harper turned her head to stare off into the distance. Everyone was quiet.

Eventually Aldar said, "As we turn off and head to the Lagoon in a few minutes, you will see the landscape becomes quite unusual. People often describe it like being on another planet. Nothing but mounds of lava rocks, as far as one can see. It's quite surreal."

Peyton glanced at Ronnie, raising one of her eyebrows.

"Hey everyone," Ronnie said. "I know we're all looking forward to the Blue Lagoon, but Peyton and I were talking. We think we need a group meeting there. Today is the last day, and we don't have a clear answer yet. The report falls on Peyton, but it's all of our responsibility. We can't leave her high and dry."

No one responded. Peyton inhaled deeply, preparing to jump in. As she slowly exhaled, Milton broke the silence. "Fine by me."

"Me too," Ariana said. "We owe it to the foundation to try to find the answer. We're getting close, I think."

"And Peyton, we'd never leave you on your own. Of course we'll help," Harper said.

"Of course," Dietrich concurred.

"I always prefer to be productive," Liev said.

Peyton smiled and mouthed, "Thank you," to Ronnie.

"Aldar, can you tell us what the plan is when we get there?" Ronnie asked.

"There is an area outside with paths where you can walk and explore part of the lagoon. It's excellent for taking photographs. You have half an hour to walk around. Then go inside and follow the sign for groups. They're expecting you. You will be directed to shower and change, everyone must shower before entering the lagoon. You will have two hours in the lagoon. I advise you stay hydrated, it is more draining than you may realize. You'll be given a plastic bracelet with a sensor, which you can use to get a drink at the bar in the lagoon. After you shower and get dressed, head to the Lava restaurant for a preordered lunch. You may stop in the gift shop on your way out. I will meet you in the front of the parking lot at 2:30."

"Great! Thanks, Aldar," Ronnie said.

"So what's the work plan?" Ariana asked.

"Yeah, we want to enjoy ourselves a bit too, eh? Peyton, what do you think?" Harper asked.

"What if we walk around and take photos and then do our own thing in the lagoon for half an hour? We can pick a spot to meet and work the rest of the time. We'll still be in the lagoon," Peyton said.

"We can continue working through lunch," Liev added.

Everyone agreed.

Peyton was relieved. *I can't believe how easy that was. I guess they take it seriously too. And they're not abandoning me. Funny how we've all become friends or something, despite all the bickering. Hmm, I'm actually going to miss them. Not just Ronnie, but all of them in a way. This ends soon. I've been so worried about the report I never thought about how I would feel.*

*   *   *

"Wow, you sure were right, Aldar. That was the wildest landscape I've ever seen. Those endless vistas of lava rocks are something," Ronnie said.

"Yeah, really was like being on another planet. Very sci-fi," Harper added.

Aldar parked the van. "Wait until you see the lagoon. Have a splendid time. I'll see you back here at 2:30."

They disembarked and started walking up the pathway, lined by walls of lava rocks. Soon they saw the entrance to the spa before them and a path to the walking part of the lagoon to their left. The tip of the lagoon was in sight.

"This must be the place Aldar suggested we look around before going inside," Ariana said.

They took a few steps forward and the lagoon revealed herself to them. There was a smattering of small lava rocks around the edge, some completely bleached from the water, and clumps of lava rocks further out mimicking small islands. The mystical water went from white to milky blue. Hills of dirt and large lava rocks covered in chartreuse moss encased the lagoon. In the distance there were large brown mountains, swirled in emerald green. It was mesmerizing.

"Oooh, look at the water color. I want to take pictures," Harper said.

"Me too. And Milton, I have to thank you again. If you didn't figure out what was making me sick I wouldn't be here, and this is just holy smokes amazing!" Ronnie said.

Milton shrugged.

"Should we do our own thing?" Ariana asked, as a few tourists passed by them. "There seem to be two pathways ahead, and we may not wind up together."

"Yeah, everyone should have a look around at their own pace," Harper said.

"Let's all meet at the front door to the spa in half an hour," Liev said.

Everyone agreed. Liev strode ahead like a soldier. Harper began skipping, with Dietrich following. Milton stayed behind, saying he was "taking it slow." Peyton, Ronnie, and Ariana walked together, following the walkway on the right.

"This is just spectacular," Ronnie said.

"I can't believe we're here. I've always wanted to see this. I never really thought I would," Peyton said.

"See, it's good to push yourself a little. But of course I'm an explorer," Ronnie said.

Peyton smiled.

"I can't wait to take a dip in it," Ariana said.

"It's magical. Like something I would have dreamed up as a kid, only better. It hardly seems real," Peyton said.

"The best things are often that way, don't you think? Better than we could have imagined," Ariana said.

Peyton nodded.

"I'm gonna start photographing it," Ronnie said, taking her phone out of her pocket. "I want to capture everything. Of course, you can never really capture everything. That's the challenge. It's hard to recreate a sensory experience. No matter how close you come, you always have to settle. A representation is never the real thing, right?" Ronnie said as she knelt on the ground to get the perfect shot.

Hmm. No it isn't. Once an experience has passed, we can only try to interpret it, Peyton thought. With that idea lingering in her mind, she stopped for a moment and slowly turned herself 360 degrees, breathing deeply, and trying to mentally record everything she saw and felt. Soon she noticed the time and said, "We should head to the spa."

*   *   *

"This robe is cozy," Harper said, rubbing her arms.

"I hope I don't trip. I'm not good in flip-flops. I feel like a penguin or something," Peyton said.

"Really? I live in 'em, back home in summer," Harper said.

"I'm not a flip-flop person either. I hate the feeling in between my toes," Ronnie said.

"Does anyone have an extra hair elastic I can borrow? I put that protective conditioner in my hair but I'd rather put it up too," Ariana said.

"I have extras," Peyton said, as she retrieved a scrunchie from her tote.

"Thank you. I love that you're always prepared," Ariana said.

Peyton smiled.

"Funny how minerals that are so good for the body are bad for hair," Harper remarked.

"I think it's a good reminder," Ariana said.

"Of what?" Harper asked.

"That perfection is a myth. There's always the possibility of something lurking, another side, an effect."

"Hmm, that's interesting," Peyton said, as she purposefully took a few small steps, careful not to fall.

"Come on, let's go meet the guys," Ronnie said.

*   *   *

"Wow, it's so warm," Peyton said, as she followed her friends into the crowded lagoon. "The hot water hitting the cold air makes a spooky layer of fog; it's wonderful."

"It's like a bath but better. I never knew if there would be motion to it but it's perfectly flat, except that little waterfall they've created over there. Boy, those kids are having fun standing under that," Ronnie said.

Everyone looked over and nodded.

"You know I didn't notice the smell out front, but once you're in it is has the faint scent of, um . . . something. Sulfur I think," Ronnie said, wiggling her nose.

"At least it's not one big fart," Ariana said with a belly laugh.

"You have to walk slowly in it," Harper said, sweeping one of her legs through the water.

Ariana jiggled her body. "Ooh, here's a hot spot."

"The water color is extraordinary. I've never seen this shade of blue before, like a milky blue," Peyton said as she cupped water in her hands and watched it slip through her fingers.

"It's actually a white color, like cream, but the sun makes it look blue," Milton said.

Harper pointed to the far side. "Yeah, look at the edges of the lava rocks, they're white. The floor too."

"Nature is the real master showman," Milton said.

Ronnie nodded. "Well said, Milton."

"I've always wanted to come here. It's supposed to be healing. People with different problems come from all over the world to be where we are right now," Peyton said, as she gently ran her hands on the water's surface.

"People can be convinced of anything. Especially if they are desperate," Liev said.

"There's science behind it. The properties of the minerals or something," Harper said.

"Yes, I'm sure it's good for some minor skin irritations, but people may get their hopes up that it's some sort of magical elixir," Liev replied.

Peyton took a breath before gently saying, "Of course you're right, but I'm guessing that a little belief in the magic of 'what if?' doesn't hurt anyone."

"Sure doesn't!" Ronnie exclaimed.

"The plan was to relax on our own and then meet. We should pick a spot," Liev said.

They all looked around. There were families walking around, kids laughing, couples holding hands on the seats along the edge, and a few groups of twenty-somethings by the bar.

"Um, how about over there, beyond that bridge?" Peyton suggested, pointing at an alcove in the farthest corner of the lagoon.

"That's good. There's a clock on the wall over there. See you all in thirty minutes," Liev said, as he began to wade away.

"I'm going to take a load off over there," Milton said, pointing to a seat lining the edge of the lagoon.

"Dietrich, you look so different without your glasses. Can you see anything?" Ronnie asked.

Dietrich squinted. "They said the minerals can scratch prescription lenses and advised taking them off. I can see but not well. I'm afraid I'm missing the view, it's quite blurry," he said.

"Don't worry. I'll get you around," Harper said. "Ooh, the facial hut is over there. Follow me, okay?"

"And then there were three," Ariana said.

"Are you two interested in trying one of those algae masks or whatever they are?" Ronnie asked.

Peyton shook her head. "But I'll go with you if you want."

"Me neither, but I'll go too," Ariana said.

"Actually how about we hit the bar instead? Grab a few drinks," Ronnie suggested.

"Sounds good," Ariana said.

They made their way to the bar and got three bottles of water. With waters in hand, they slowly started heading to the far corner of the lagoon, where they were to meet the others.

"Liev is so stubborn. I feel real bad for him being sick, which he obviously wants to keep private, but people come to thermal baths in Iceland from all over the world for their healing value. He just dismisses it. He loves shooting down ideas he doesn't understand," Ronnie said.

"The first time he was sick, he only did conventional treatments. People suggested alternative therapies, but he wouldn't hear of it," Ariana said.

"He's all science all the time," Ronnie said.

"Yes, but this time around he was different. The science was bleak, and so he tried many things," Ariana said.

"Really?" Peyton asked.

"He's tried Eastern treatments from herbs to acupuncture. At one point he had a problem with his skin, and he even visited a Turkish bath or something in Spain," Ariana replied.

Peyton's eyes widened. "He did?"

"Unfortunately it didn't help, or at least not much," Ariana said.

"If he's tried all of these things, why does he put them down? He must believe they have some value or at least that it's possible," Peyton said.

"His health is an impossibility he can't solve. I think believing in possibility is too painful for him. And no doubt he feels foolish for trying things that didn't work," Ariana said.

"Isn't that what scientists do? They try things that don't work until they find what does work. It's the nature of experimentation," Ronnie said.

"You're very clever, Ronnie," Ariana said.

"People can't always see things clearly when it's personal," Peyton said.

"Don't let Liev hear you say that! He'd take it the wrong way and give us a lecture on scientific neutrality or something," Ronnie said.

Peyton laughed. "I do still think that, well . . ."

"What do you think?" Ronnie asked.

"We shouldn't underestimate the power of believing in 'what if?', believing in possibility."

*   *   *

When Peyton, Ronnie, and Ariana arrived at the alcove, they sat on the ledge, and Peyton lifted her legs up to watch them float at the surface of the water.

"I feel incredibly lucky to be here," she said.

"Me too. It's really soothing," Ariana said.

"It's just so beautiful here. Look at those lava rocks. It looks like yellow and green moss ran across them, blown by the wind, and then suddenly froze in place," Peyton said.

Ronnie smiled. "Hey there, you're starting to sound like an artist."

Peyton pursed her lips.

"I think it's the juxtaposition that makes it so spectacular," Ronnie said.

Peyton smiled. "See, you have the real art eye. What exactly do you mean about the juxtaposition?"

"Well, there's the light-colored water up against the black lava rocks, totally dramatic. And the water is hot, the air cold. Then with those mountains in the distance, it's just all about contrast. The power you can unleash juxtaposing disparate elements is something you learn about doing collage work. Makes all the difference. Each element looks totally different than it would without the other elements," Ronnie said.

Hmm, Peyton thought. *Juxtaposition. Contrast. Disparate elements. The welcome packet called this place the land of fire and ice. I wonder if that's what they meant.* Before she could say anything, Milton and Liev were strolling over. Liev's face was covered in white goop.

"Uh, hi. So you got a facial treatment?" Ariana asked.

"It's a cleansing mask. I think the fifteen minutes have passed," he said as he splashed water on his face, rubbing away the mask.

"You have a little behind your left ear," Ronnie said.

"Ah," he mumbled, as he continued washing his face.

Harper and Dietrich approached, hand in hand. Peyton and Ronnie smiled at each other.

"We're not late, are we? Had to guide this poor guy around," Harper said.

"You're not late," Ariana said. "Did you get facial treatments? Liev did."

"I only got the cleansing mask. It's important to keep your skin clean," Liev said.

Harper giggled. "We got the algae mask. My skin feels great."

"Did you like it, Dietrich?" Ronnie asked.

"It was different," he replied, twitching his nose.

Everyone laughed.

"Okay, shall we get started? Who's first?" Liev asked.

"Actually, Ronnie just said something a few minutes ago that got me thinking. We may be close to the answer," Peyton said.

There in the farthest corner of the enchanting waters of the Blue Lagoon, Peyton shared her ideas. The group was engrossed in conversation for the next hour and a half, and continued on through lunch. By the time they went to the gift shop, Peyton's heart raced, not with anxiety, but with hope.

*   *   *

"Time to wake up, everyone. We're back at the manor," Aldar said.

Peyton squinted, adjusting to the light. There were yawns, outstretched arms, and slumped bodies trying to straighten up.

"Well, look at that. Even I conked out this time," Milton said.

"People often don't realize while they're in it, but the mineral bath is draining. Glad you all got some rest," Aldar said.

Everyone gathered their belongings and dragged themselves out of the van.

"Oooh, that cool air will wake ya up," Ronnie said.

"What a splendid day," Ariana said, before covering her mouth to yawn.

Harper stretched her arms. "Hope we can reenergize."

"We'll need the strong stuff at afternoon tea," Liev said.

"I'm going to my room. See you all at tea," Harper said.

"See you all at tea," Dietrich said.

As everyone made their way inside, Peyton grabbed Ronnie.

"What a day!" Ronnie exclaimed.

"Yeah, it was great. I just wanted to tell you I'm not going to make it to tea. I need to type up notes for today and review all of my notes before the last session."

"We're on the cusp," Ronnie said.

Peyton smiled.

"See you later. Good luck!" Ronnie said.

"Thanks."

＊　　＊　　＊

Peyton hung up her coat and put her tote bag in the closet. *There's no time to waste*, she thought, flipping her laptop on. She typed quickly, trying to record as many details from the day as possible. *Time to review it all.* She got a notebook and pen to jot down things that might be important. Beginning with her notes from the first day, Peyton carefully examined each day's notes, interrogating her observations, impressions, and the process the group had followed. She noted critical moments and turning points, as well as the quiet comments that slipped under the group's radar. She held the notebook in her hands, staring at a list of words and phrases. *Could it be? Could it be that simple?*

✳   ✳   ✳

Peyton bounded into the Japanese Garden room, laptop and notebook in hand. She leaned against the door to catch her breath. Everyone was laughing.

"Hey, there. You okay?" Ronnie asked.

"Yeah, I raced over here. I'm so sorry I'm late," Peyton replied.

"That's okay. Ariana entertained us. Had us in hysterics," Harper said.

"She's quite funny," Liev said, his cheeks flushed.

"She does a great impression of the Queen," Milton added.

Peyton smiled and filled the empty seat next to Ronnie. "I don't want to break up the fun."

"Work now, play later," Ariana said.

"Should we continue from where we left off at lunch? We were making progress," Dietrich suggested.

"Yes, we were. I'm sure Ronnie told you that's why I skipped the tea. I used the time to review all of my notes. I think I understand now. May I explain it to you?" Peyton asked.

Everyone nodded and sat quietly as Peyton told them what she thought the answer was. When she finished, smiles swept across their faces.

"We have it," Liev said.

Chapter 14

*　　*　　*

Peyton looked at herself in the mirror, thinking, *The packet said to dress in cocktail attire for the final celebration dinner. I hope this is okay. A simple black dress is always appropriate, right?* She rubbed the side of her dress to smooth away any wrinkles and headed to dinner.

She walked downstairs slowly, running her hand along the banister, appreciating every detail. *Enjoy yourself tonight. Savor the remaining moments in this wondrous place with these wondrous people.*

As she approached the grand hall she met up with a few others. Ariana was wearing a floor-length, hot pink dress and gold high-heels.

"Wow. You look amazing," Peyton said.

"Thank you. I figured I'd go for it for the final soiree. You look lovely too," Ariana said.

Peyton smiled.

They walked into the dining hall, which was glowing from an abundance of candlelight. Ariana headed over to join Liev and some others while Peyton looked for her friends.

"Over here," Harper called.

Wow, everyone looks so nice, Peyton thought as she joined her friends.

"You look terrific," Ronnie said.

"Oh, thanks. You should see Ariana," Peyton replied.

"We noticed her walk in. Show-stopping dress," Harper said.

"We clean up real nice," Ronnie said.

Peyton admired the details on the table—votive candles, white flowers, and champagne flutes filled to the brim. She glanced around. "That's what's different, no buffet."

"It's a sit-down dinner tonight. But there's a bread basket to tide you over," Milton said, as he buttered a popover.

"Oh, there's Ms. Goodright," Peyton said.

They all shifted in their seats and looked at Ms. Goodright. She walked to the center of the room, holding a glass of champagne, as the light from the chandeliers and candles glistened against her black sequinned gown. She stood, literally sparkling from head to toe.

"Good evening, everyone," she said.

The chatter halted, and a sea of smiling faces turned toward her.

"I hope you had a wonderful and productive last day. It has been our sincere pleasure to host you. I have a deep fondness for each of you, and I hope our paths cross again. We know how hard you've worked and the sacrifices you've made to spend this time here."

Peyton looked around the room, catching a glimpse of Liev, as Ms. Goodright continued.

"Tonight we are treating you to a special thank-you dinner. Please join me in showing our appreciation to Juliette and the entire staff."

Everyone clapped.

"We do hope you will make use of our facilities after dinner. Relish your time together and celebrate all you accomplished here. Please note that, as indicated in your packet, there are extended hours for breakfast tomorrow to accommodate travel schedules. The staff is happy to prepare takeaway meals or snacks as well.

Without further ado, I shall turn the floor over to our staff, who will now serve dinner. Please be well on your journey. We hope you will carry us in your memory, as we will treasure you in ours. Cheers."

Everyone held their champagne glasses up and said, "Cheers." They sipped their bubbly as Ms. Goodright exited the room, twinkling the entire way.

The staff descended upon the tables, serving the first course: a slow-cooked egg with vegetables and herbs. Everyone marveled at the beautiful plates. Peyton cut into the silken egg. "This is delicious," she said. The festivities continued as the sounds of gleeful chatter and champagne corks popping, flooded the dining hall. After they finished their beef filet, shellfish soup, and mushroom tartlet entrees, the staff walked around each table offering coffee and tea. Just as Peyton said, "I don't think I can eat another bite," dessert was served: a trio of sorbets with meringue chards served on ice blocks.

"Wow, this is so cool," Ronnie said.

"Really reminds you you're in Iceland, eh?" Harper added.

They all agreed.

During dessert, some people milled about the room, stopping at friends' tables to talk. After a while, people started heading to the pub.

Milton licked the last drops of sorbet off his spoon and looked at the others. "Well, I'm done. Should we join them?"

"You bet ya," Ronnie said.

"It's our last night, better make the most of it," Harper said, rubbing Dietrich's arm.

Our last night. That makes me feel so sad, Peyton thought.

Everyone stood up. Peyton stopped for a moment and slowly turned around 360 degrees.

"You coming?" Ronnie asked.

"Uh huh. Just want to remember the way it looked tonight," she replied.

"Take it in. I'll wait for you," Ronnie said.

"Actually, I have to run to my room to get something. I'll meet you there."

*   *   *

Peyton could hear boisterous laughter all the way from the top of the stairs leading down to the pub. She walked into the crowded, hot room holding the bottle of wine she'd been keeping for days.

"There you are!" Ronnie called from the bar.

Peyton shimmied her way through the crowd, exchanging smiles and hellos on her way.

"I'm getting a bottle of water. You want anything?" Ronnie asked.

Peyton shook her head. "Just grab a wine opener, please. Where's Liev?"

"In the game room. Our whole group is in there," Ronnie replied.

Peyton got a couple of wine glasses, and the two women made their way into the game room. Ariana, barefoot, with her shoes strewn on a bench, was engaged in a Ping-Pong battle with an Austrian musician. Peyton giggled. "Funny to see everyone so formally dressed up, just casually hanging out down here."

Peyton spotted Liev in the far corner talking with a few men. She headed straight for him.

"Hi, everyone," she said, joining Liev's conversation.

"Peyton, we were taking bets on who is going to win this round. What do you think?" Liev asked.

Peyton glanced over. "Ariana looks determined. My money is on her."

"Agreed," Liev said.

Peyton lifted her hand, showing Liev the wine.

"What's this?" he asked, taking the bottle.

"I remembered you're a wine connoisseur. A few days ago, after your lecture, I asked Diego if he had a special bottle of red wine. I wanted to give it to you that night to tell you how impressed I was by your talk, but it didn't work out. I've been holding on to it."

"Waiting for someday," he said, before carefully examining the bottle. "Shall we try it?"

Peyton nodded.

Liev uncorked the bottle and poured a little into the two glasses Peyton was holding. He swirled the wine in his glass and smelled it. "Cheers," he said, clinking her glass.

Peyton took a sip. She thought it was delicious, but didn't want to say anything, having no real knowledge of wine.

Liev smiled. "Very smooth. An excellent wine indeed. Thank you."

"My pleasure," Peyton said.

"I'm glad to have met you here. You are my favorite sociologist," he said.

Peyton opened her mouth but was interrupted by an explosion of cheers. Everyone in the room was clapping and hollering. Ariana won her match.

"Who is to play the winner?" Liev called over.

"Let's all play together," Ariana said.

"What do you mean?" someone asked.

"It's really fun. Everyone stands around the table. The two people on the ends have the paddles. They each take a shot, and then we all move down the table and they pass the paddles on to the next people. The idea is to see how long you can go, keeping the ball in air," Ariana said.

Liev put his wine down and unbuttoned the top buttons of his shirt. "It's hot in here," he said.

Others removed their shawls, their high-heeled shoes; one woman even took her stockings off. People gathered around the table with Ariana and Liev each at one end. Peyton and Milton were the only people from their group not at the table.

"Milton, come play," Ariana said.

Milton shrugged and joined the group.

"Peyton, come on," Liev said.

"Oh, I'm not good at this. I don't want to mess it up," she replied.

"No one cares. It's for fun," Ariana said.

Peyton joined the group. Ariana took the first shot. Liev hit back, handing the paddle to Ronnie, and everyone kept moving. People were laughing so heartily they barely noticed when Peyton hit the ball so hard it flew to the other side of the room. Someone retrieved it and they continued on. They kept the ball in the air until it was Peyton's turn, and she hit it down into the net instead of over. While Dietrich retrieved the ball, Liev took the paddle and showed Peyton how to gently hit it over the net. They continued playing, pushing each other around in a hot, sweaty circle. Everyone cheered when Peyton hit the ball over the net on her third try. They were so excited, Harper missed the next shot. Soon they were a well-oiled machine, circling the table with ease. They continued playing, beads of sweat glistening on their skin. As they moved around the table, Peyton studied everyone's smiling faces. She grinned ear to ear, her heart racing. Just like when she was a little girl, she was a part of something.

※　　　※　　　※

Peyton noticed it was past midnight. She leaned over to Ronnie. "I'm going to my room."

"Oh, but we're having such a great time," Ronnie said.

"I still have to write the final report."

"Oh gee, I forgot about that. I'll see you at breakfast."

"See you at breakfast," Peyton said.

She stopped under the archway between the bar and game room, looking at her friends. *We'll probably never all be together again. It's going to be hard to go back to my normal life, knowing these superheroes exist.*

Once upstairs, Peyton decided to wander around a bit before heading to her room. She passed by the paintings that had captivated her on the first day. She stood before one depicting human shapes in the mountains. She smiled, thinking about the faces in the rocks at the tectonic plates.

"Having a last look?" a voice said.

Peyton jumped.

"I'm sorry. I didn't mean to startle you."

"Oh, Diego. Hello. Yes, I'm just trying to soak it all in. This place is magical. I can't believe I have to leave in the morning."

"May I say, you seem right at home? I knew you would," Diego said.

"You were right. Actually, before you came along I was thinking . . ."

"Yes?" he prodded.

"Well, it's going to be really hard to say goodbye to everyone, including you."

Diego smiled. "Goodbyes are always difficult. But if you think about, it means your time was well spent."

Peyton smiled. "You always cast a new light on things."

"Perhaps you have something else on your mind, too?" Diego inquired.

"The final report. I still have to write it. I think we came up with the answer, but . . ."

"Please, let me show you something special, for a little inspiration."

"Okay," she said, following him toward the library.

"Do you remember the secret doorway I showed you?" he asked.

"Uh huh."

"I told you it goes up to the roof. Let me take you. It's unlike anything you have seen before."

"Oh, I'm actually notoriously afraid of heights," Peyton said.

"That is because you look down. We will look up."

"Well, I am trying to get better about my fears," she mumbled.

"It will be cold. I'll get blankets from the back room. Please wait a moment," he said.

Peyton waited, looking around the exquisite library, thinking about all of the conversations that had taken place within its walls.

Diego returned with a pile of blankets. "Follow me."

They entered the secret doorway. Diego pulled the string, illuminating the small space. Peyton followed him up the winding staircase. At the top, he opened a door. "Remember, look up."

Peyton followed him onto the roof, tilting her head up. It was breathtaking. There were stars as far as the eye could see.

"Come here," Diego said, as he placed a blanket on the floor. "Lie down for the best view."

Peyton lay on the blanket and Diego placed another blanket on top of her before lying down himself.

"You were right. It's spectacular. I've never seen so many stars before," Peyton said.

"They look like little sparks lighting up the sky, don't you think?" Diego asked.

"Uh huh."

"Some of those sparks contain entire worlds. Like some of the teeniest sparks of creativity this week contain the greatest insights. And like the spark inside of you, inside of us all. Entire worlds of possibility and wonder."

Peyton smiled, looking up at the night sky, thinking about Diego's words and everything she experienced in this place.

After a little while they returned to the library to warm up. Diego said, "I'm going to put the blankets back and turn in. Would you like me to walk you back to the other building?"

"I think I'm going to stay in here for a little while," Peyton replied.

"Good night," he said.

"Good night. And thank you," she said as he left.

Peyton looked around the room. She thought about Diego's words. *Some of those sparks contain entire worlds. Entire worlds of possibility and wonder.* She sat down at a computer and opened a new document. After a deep breath, she wrote the final report. She read it over, smiled, and emailed it to herself and to Ms. Goodright.

Chapter 15

*   *   *

Peyton was still trying to wake up when she arrived at the sparsely attended breakfast. The grand hall was quiet, but she imagined it echoed with the joyful sounds from the night before. She grabbed a bowl of oatmeal and joined her friends.

"Good morning," Ronnie said.

"What time did you all leave the pub last night?" Peyton asked.

Harper yawned. "Oh golly, just a few hours ago, I suppose."

"Even you, Milton?" Peyton asked.

"You bet. But I'm fueling up now," he said as he took the last bite of a croissant.

"He's stocking up before he goes home to his wife. He had two plates loaded with ham, eggs, and pastries," Harper said.

Milton blushed. "My wife is going to put me on a diet when I get home."

"I'm going to miss our breakfasts," Harper said.

Milton smiled and stood up. "Well, I don't want to be late for the van to the airport."

"Safe journey," Ronnie said.

"I'll miss you," Peyton said.

Milton shrugged, and then paused and bowed his head forward. "Goodbye folks."

"And then there were four," Harper said.

Peyton sighed and took a bite of oatmeal.

"Did you get the report done?" Ronnie asked.

"Uh huh," Peyton said, before taking another bite. "Where are Ariana and Liev?"

"They already left. They said to say goodbye. Liev wanted me to thank you for the wine and tell you it was one of the best he's ever had," Ronnie said.

Peyton looked down, smiling.

"I'm going to meet up with Ariana when she's in DC working on her grant," Ronnie continued.

"That's great," Peyton said.

"Harper, do you think we should get going?" Dietrich asked.

"Yeah, I suppose so," Harper replied.

"You two off to the airport?" Ronnie asked.

Harper shook her head. "I rented a car. We're traveling together. We've gotten close, and we aren't ready to leave."

"Wow, that's great. Where are you heading?" Ronnie asked.

"We're gonna jump on the Ring Road," Harper said. "The scenery is supposed to be spectacular."

"We'll definitely stop in Akureyri for a couple days. One of the travel guides named it the best place to see in Europe," Dietrich added.

"He feels better if he can plan something," Harper said.

Dietrich blushed.

"So Peyton, I guess it's just you and me heading to the airport in the next shuttle," Ronnie said.

"Actually, I'm not going to the airport either. Last night when I got back to my room I looked up that glacier tour I told you about. Turns out there was still room, so I took the plunge and booked it. I'm meeting the bus in Reykjavik later."

"That's awesome!" Ronnie exclaimed. "I'm thrilled for you."

"I figured today was better than someday," Peyton said, surprised when her eyes suddenly swelled with tears.

"Good for you," Harper said.

"Yes," Dietrich said. "I guess none of us are quite the same."
Everyone smiled.

Peyton turned to Ronnie, "This is really hard. I'm going to miss you so much. I never expected to make such a great friend."

"We're pals for life! I'll see you on social media. And I want to visit you in the fall. I know the foliage is spectacular in Vermont. Maybe it will inspire a new installation. Can you put me up?"

Peyton beamed. "That would be great."

"Well, we better finish up, seems we all have places to go," Ronnie said.

Yup, places to go, Peyton thought.

*   *   *

Peyton arrived at the front desk, luggage in hand.

"Fana, I was hoping to say goodbye to Ms. Goodright. Do you know where she is?"

"She's out back in our little greenhouse."

"Thank you."

"Please, leave your luggage. I'll have a driver bring it to the van," Fana said.

"Oh, I'm not going to the airport. I was going to call a cab to take me into Reykjavik."

"Nonsense. It would be our pleasure to have one of the drivers take you."

"Thank you," Peyton said, placing her suitcase on the floor.

She walked outside and headed to the back of the manor, finding Ms. Goodright elbow deep in soil.

"Hello there, Peyton."

"I don't want to bother you."

"It's no bother," Ms. Goodright said.

"I just wanted to thank you. I've had such a wonderful time."

"It was our pleasure to have you," Ms. Goodright said.

"Thank you again. I see you're busy," Peyton said.

"I'm just planting seeds. That's what I do really. You see, I'm a gardener by nature. I plant seeds. It's exciting to see how they grow."

"It must take patience," Peyton said.

"The best things do."

"May I ask you something before I leave?" Peyton asked.

"Of course."

"The next group coming tomorrow, will they be answering the same question?"

Ms. Goodright smiled. "Yes."

"How many have there been?" Peyton asked.

"Two thousand five hundred and forty-seven."

"The number on the welcome packet," Peyton said.

"Precisely. I imagine when we can think of a more important question, we'll ask it."

Peyton smiled. "Thank you for everything."

✳   ✳   ✳

"Well it looks like it's you and me again," Aldar said, as he opened the van door for Peyton.

Peyton sat in the van. *Ms. Goodright is unlike anyone I've met before. A gardener, indeed. She is clever.* She turned to see Crystal Manor one last time. As it got smaller in the rearview mirror, she felt a mix of emotions—happiness, sadness, and anticipation. She took out her phone and opened her email. There was a message from Harper with an attachment. Peyton opened it to see the group selfie of all of them at the top of Gullfoss waterfall. She inhaled, overcome with joy, and tears flowed down her cheeks. *Look at each of them. I'm so grateful for what they taught me.* She wiped her eyes and opened the email she had sent Ms. Goodright.

Dear Ms. Goodright,

I want to express my profound gratitude to the Goodright Foundation for this extraordinary experience. I don't think any of us will ever be same. When my group heard the question we needed to answer, we were mystified. Honestly, I didn't know why I was invited here. Eventually, it all made sense.

Each one of us was needed in order to arrive at the answer. You reminded us to challenge our assumptions, to be unafraid to change our minds. For me, separating my observations from my impressions proved to be an important step. Admittedly, I formed early judgments about people in my group. In the end, I learned from each of my new friends. I'd like to share what they taught me.

Initially, I thought both Ariana and Liev were insufferable, but Ariana ended up teaching us more than perhaps anyone. Early on she said that we needed to focus on the question itself. As it turned out she was right, even though we didn't realize it until the very end. Ariana was quick to point out that sometimes people don't see what's right in front of their faces. I'm embarrassed to admit, I failed to appreciate her unique vantage point, struggles, and strengths. As for answering the question, not seeing what's right in front of you turned out to be a recurring theme. For example, we played one game where we all picked fruits until we ran out of ideas. Nobody said orange. Ariana noticed that many people in the group had had orange juice to drink that morning. Finally, she also always brought in a broader perspective than whatever the group was talking about. Whether we were talking about the nootka lupine spreading too far, the number of continents, or environmental pollution, she made us consider a global perspective. Ariana gave us the ability to focus on what was right in front of us *and* to broaden out.

Then there's Harper, a true free spirit. Not everyone took her seriously at first, but she forced us to look at things differently. Because of her, we couldn't even conclusively determine what should count as a shape and what shouldn't. She reminded us to be flexible in our thinking. When she, Liev, and Dietrich were sparring about the sciences and arts, she cautioned us that just because we see a Jackson Pollock painting as splatter on a canvas that a child could do, it doesn't mean we're right, or that we even understand what we're seeing. Each discipline is valuable.

Speaking of Dietrich, he taught me that it's okay to change our minds and challenge our assumptions. He started out with such certainty that his perspective was right, but by the end, he was open to all perspectives. This proved important personally, too, as I learned new things about my friends and was forced to consider that there had been much I wasn't seeing.

Then of course there was Liev, who I also judged harshly early on. Although he and Dietrich argued incessantly, they weren't as different as they thought. They were both actually taking the same fixed position. Liev was insistent that it was a scientific research question. Although not in the way he expected, that thinking helped us find the answer. I'll explain shortly.

Milton was the real question mark in our group. None of us could figure out what an elderly, retired farmer could possibly contribute to a group of scholars and artists. I don't even think Milton knew. As it turns out, Milton's experiential knowledge was invaluable. He was the only person who figured out what was making Ronnie sick. Through careful, systematic observations, he developed a hunch that proved to be correct. If not for Milton, Ronnie wouldn't have come to the Blue Lagoon.

That brings me to my dear friend, Ronnie. She always taught us to look at things from different angles and distances: the close-up and distant views. She'd take dozens of photographs of one rock to begin to capture it, knowing reality can ultimately only be interpreted and represented, never copied. Her biggest contribution was at the Blue Lagoon when she explained that the juxtaposition of elements in the landscape gave them their meaning and made them bigger than the sum of their parts. That, we realized, was a metaphor for our group.

And then there's me. I mustered the courage to push past my comfort zone and tap into new leadership skills. Liev's insistence it was a research question made me consider how I would approach a research question in my own field. That's when I suggested the group bring in other perspectives from literature in our individual fields, which proved to be a turning point. Not only did we elicit new ideas, but we also learned how to work together respectfully.

I'm sorry if this is a bit of a ramble. I know you wanted a concise response. So, here it is. The answer is:

Start with the question itself. Observe carefully and systematically, questioning what you normally take for granted. Separate your observations or other data from your impressions. Apply different perspectives, including a micro-level frame and a broad, macro-level frame. Remain flexible—you may need to adapt along the way. Challenge your assumptions. Value every discipline without privileging any. Value experiential or lay knowledge. Work collaboratively and respectfully. Bring in voices from the relevant literature, looking for synergies or dissonances, because the sum is bigger than the parts. Context matters: how pieces of information sit in relation to one another creates meaning. Reality can never be fully captured, but we can do our best to interpret and represent it. The entire process may be messy, and you may have to adjust as you go. And above all, as I noted from the outset, always stay focused on the question itself.

Because you see, in the end we realized you weren't asking for the answer to one question. You were asking: What is the answer to every question?

FURTHER ENGAGEMENT

DISCUSSION AND HOMEWORK QUESTIONS

1. The group has several discussions over the course of the novel (for example, about the number seven, shapes, fruits). Select one of these conversations. What do we learn from this scene?

2. At the Blue Lagoon Ronnie says that reality can never be fully captured, but we can do our best to interpret and represent it. Peyton later includes this in the final report. What do you think this means?

3. Metaphors and symbolism are used throughout the novel. Pick and discuss one example.

4. Certain words and phrases are repeated throughout the novel (for example, *Ping-Pong, spark, someday is dangerous*). Select a word or phrase that comes up more than once and discuss the different contexts in which the word or phrase is used and what you think the significance is.

5. As Ariana points out, the number of continents is cultural, not universal. Look this up online and discuss what it teaches us about perspective.

6. Intersectionality theory, which was developed by Black feminist scholars, examines the intersections of race, class, and gender as paths of privilege and oppression. Ariana exemplifies this when she talks about being "forced to negotiate multiple realities." What does she mean by this? What are other examples of this in academia or society more generally?

7. Fiction allows for the representation of interiority, that is, what a character is thinking. Throughout the novel we see Peyton, Liev, and Dietrich's interior dialogue. Select one of these characters and discuss what we learn about them from their interior dialogue.

RESEARCH ACTIVITIES

For activities 1–5 select a research topic you're interested in studying.

1. **Literature Review.** Conduct a preliminary literature review (six to eight peer-reviewed sources). First, read, annotate, and summarize each source. Next, synthesize the literature by looking for synergies and dissonances. If you'd like more information about literature reviews, here are a few suggested readings:

   Efron, S. E., & Ravid, R. (2019). *Writing the literature review: A practical guide.* New York: Guilford Press.
   Leavy, P. (2017). *Research design: Quantitative, qualitative, mixed methods, arts-based, and community-based participatory research approaches.* New York: Guilford Press.
   Ling Pan, M. (2017). *Preparing literature reviews: Qualitative and quantitative approaches* (5th ed.). Oxon, UK: Routledge.

2. **Concept Maps.** After everyone in Peyton's group researched problem solving in their fields, they came together and created a visual representation of their findings—a concept map. Pick a key concept or phenomenon under investigation and place it at the center of your map. Then use the findings from your literature review to create a concept map. Lump similar pieces of information together. Use lines/arrows/dotted lines to show relationships between different pieces of literature. Use different colors if it's helpful.

3. **Observations/Impressions.** Remember when Peyton began typing her notes after the first group meeting? She separated her observations and impressions. Collect a small sample of data using a qualitative research method (for example, ethnography, interview, content analysis). Analyze the data by pulling out key words/phrases, repetitions, and so forth. Create a two-column list, one with your direct observations from the data and the second with your impressions (for example, what you think it means, how data are connected, the significance) just like Peyton did.

4. **Applying Macro and Micro Frames.** Macro-level theories look at large-scale processes and institutions. Micro-level theories look at small-scale interactions or experiences at

the individual or small-group level. For example, a particular macro-level theory about gender and communication may explore how power dynamics operate at the institutional level, whereas a particular micro-level theory may examine patterns of interaction among small groups. By applying both types of theories you can look at the dynamics in a specific group and situate that discussion within a larger context. Select two theories that come up in your literature review, one micro-theory and one macro-theory (if you need to, search for additional literature). Take the data you have collected and analyze them using each of the two theories. What do you learn from each way of looking at the data?

5. ***Conceptualizing Group Projects.*** There are numerous ways of building group projects, from general team approaches to specific designs. For example, community-based approaches involve collaboratively working with community partners, at times including an established community-based organization, during all phases of the project beginning with problem identification. Participatory approaches invite research participants to be involved with designing and carrying out research beyond serving as sources of data. Transdisciplinary approaches involve researchers from multiple disciplines coming together to create a framework that transcends individual disciplines—much like Peyton's group. Let's say you're planning to conduct a team, community-based, participatory, or transdisciplinary project on your topic. Identify the relevant stakeholders who should comprise your team. Relevant stakeholders are those groups of people who have a vested interest in the topic. Consider what disciplinary bodies of knowledge are needed and what experiential or lay knowledge is needed. For example, a project about bullying in elementary schools might include educators, sociologists, school administration, students, parents, after-school staff, cafeteria staff, and school bus drivers.

6. ***Small-Group Collaboration Activity.*** Remember when Peyton's group finally learned to work together in the library, as they researched their fields and looked for connections? Respect and valuing each other's perspectives was key. With this in mind, get into groups of four to five. Select a research topic that everyone has some interest in and, together, define the problem you would tackle. You're not actually going to

carry out this research, but as a group, come up with a plan for how you would collaboratively study it so that the division of labor is fair and everyone's talents are best used.

7. ***Discourse or Conversation Analysis.*** Select one of the group conversation scenes and use it as data. Perform discourse or conversation analysis on the scene, analyzing the content of what is said, the flow or back-and-forth of the dialogue, displays of power or hierarchy, nonverbal or other gestures, and anything else that you notice.

CREATIVE WRITING ACTIVITIES

1. Pick up on Peyton's story. Write about her experience on the glacier tour or a day in her life a year later. Think about how she might have changed.

2. Write the story of Dietrich and Harper's road trip.

3. In the novel we are never exposed to Ronnie's, Milton's, Ariana's, or Harper's interiority. Select one of them and write a scene that takes place in his or her room at Crystal Manor and includes interior dialogue.

4. Imagine the final report is in the hands of one of the other characters. Rewrite it from that person's perspective.

5. Take one of the minor characters (for example, Ms. Goodright, Fana, Aldar) and write his or her story.

6. Early in the novel Peyton is trying to figure out how she was invited to Crystal Manor. She wonders if it's because of an op-ed she wrote for the *New York Times*, but she never explains what it was about. Write the op-ed.

7. Imagine the characters are reunited a year later. Write the conversation they have.

Acknowledgments

B ooks are never the result of one person's work, but rather represent the work and generosity of many.

First and foremost, I am profoundly grateful to my publisher, editor extraordinaire, and dear friend, C. Deborah Laughton. I will never be able to thank you enough for your belief in this project. I love working with you.

I extend a spirited thank you to the world-class team at The Guilford Press. I'm truly honored to work with you. In particular, thank you to Bob Matloff, Marian Robinson, Lucy Baker, Andrea Sargent, Andrea Lansing, Anne Patota, Katherine Sommer, Laura Specht Patchkofsky, Judith Grauman, Oliver Sharpe, Katherine Lieber, Paul Gordon, and Carly DaSilva. And an extra special thank you to Seymour Weingarten. This was an unconventional project for Guilford, and I'm indebted to you for taking a chance on it.

Special thanks to my assistant and treasured friend, Shalen Lowell. I wouldn't have been able to devote myself to this book if you weren't keeping so many other balls in the air. Thank you!

I'm also appreciative of my friends and colleagues for lending their support. Special thanks to Pam DeSantis, Sandra Faulkner, Ally Field, Libby Hatlan, Jessica Smartt Gullion, Rebecca Kamen, Eve Spangler, and Adrienne Trier-Bieniek. Mort Mathers, you're my favorite farmer. Thank you for writing a draft of the chicken scene. You're the best! Laurel Richardson, the discussion of seven was inspired by your gorgeous book *Seven Minutes from Home*. I'm grateful for the inspiration and your unfailing support. Thank you to Robin Patric Clair for your wonderful insights about the seven conversation. Melissa Anyiwo, a special thank you for watching Madeline so that I could go to Austria. This book was inspired by that trip. I owe you one! And my eternal gratitude to Celine Boyle, my friend, confidante, and writing buddy. There are no words to thank you for your invaluable feedback on every page of the manuscript, your enthusiasm, and so much more. Thank you!

I'm also grateful to my family. Daisy, my little best friend, thanks for the tail of joy. Madeline, you are my heart. Mark, you are the best spouse anyone could have. Thank you for believing in this book and in me.

Finally, this novel is dedicated to Salzburg Global Seminar Group 547. I will never forget our time together in Austria, at the *Sound of Music* house. Sharing that experience with you was one of the greatest privileges of my life. You all inspired me so much that I wrote the outline to this novel in Vienna, the day after we parted. Life is much sweeter knowing there are superheroes in the world.

About the Author

Patricia Leavy, PhD, is an independent sociologist and former Chair of Sociology and Criminology and Founding Director of Gender Studies at Stonehill College in Easton, Massachusetts. She is the author, coauthor, or editor of over 25 books including fiction and nonfiction, and the creator and editor of seven book series. Known for her commitment to public scholarship, she is frequently contacted by the U.S. national news media and has regular blogs for *The Creativity Post* and *We Are the Real Deal*. She is also co-founder and co-editor-in-chief of the journal *Art/Research International*. Dr. Leavy has received numerous awards for her work in the field of research methods, including the New England Sociologist of the Year Award from the New England Sociological Association, the Special Achievement Award from the American Creativity Association, the Egon Guba Memorial Keynote Lecture Award from the American Educational Research Association Qualitative Special Interest Group, the Special Career Award from the International Congress of Qualitative Inquiry, the Significant Contribution to Educational Measurement and Research Methodology Award from the American Educational Research Association, and the Distinguished Contributions Outside the Profession Award from the National Art Education Association. In 2016, Mogul, a global women's empowerment platform, named her an "Influencer." In 2018, she was honored by the National Women's Hall of Fame and SUNY New Paltz established the annual Patricia Leavy Award for Art and Social Justice. Dr. Leavy delivers invited lectures and keynote addresses at universities and conferences. Her website is *www.patricialeavy.com*.